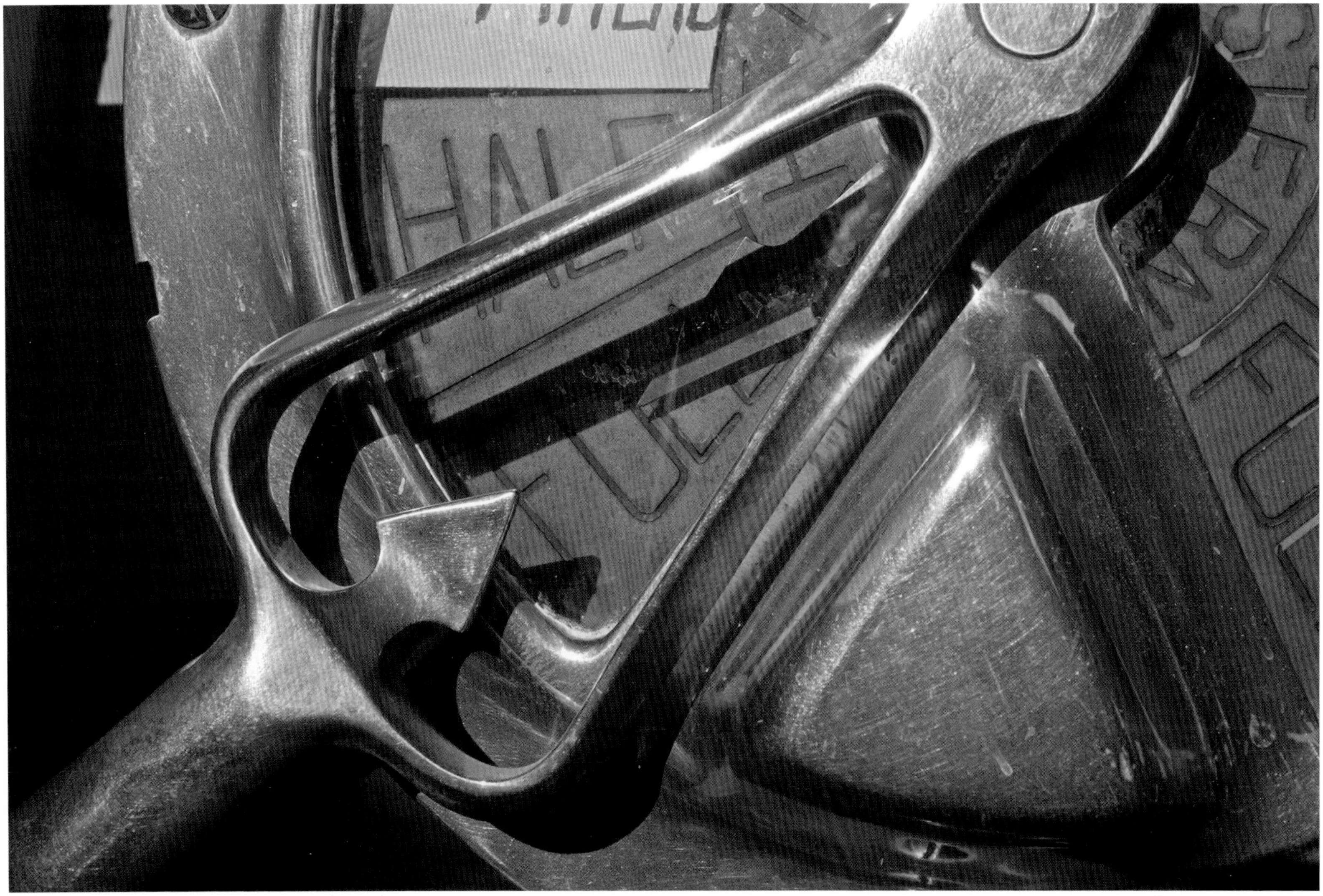

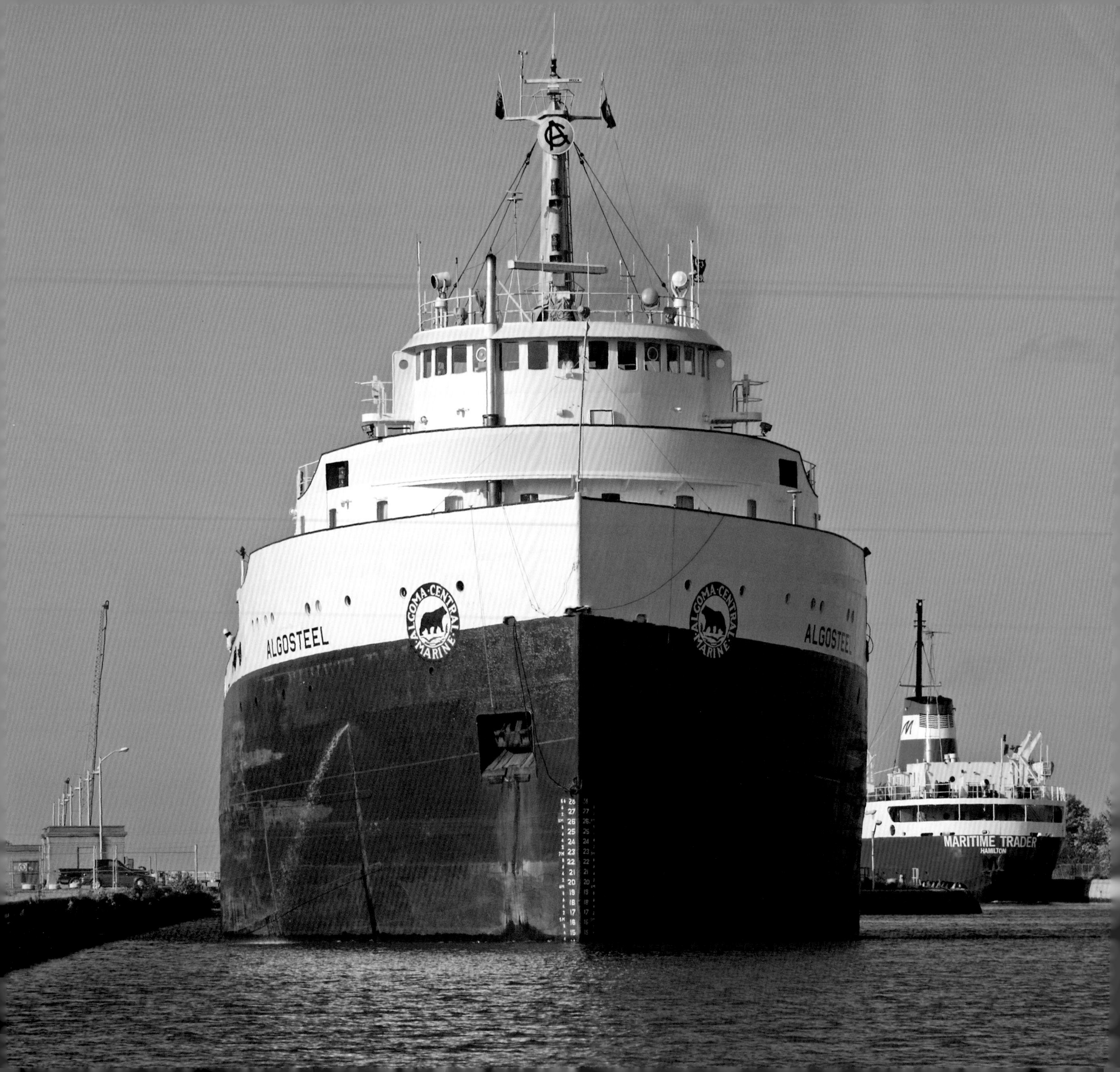
ALGOSTEEL
ALGOMA CENTRAL MARINE
ALGOSTEEL
ALGOMA CENTRAL MARINE
MARITIME TRADER
HAMILTON

Second Edition

Greg McDonnell
LAKE BOATS

THE ENDURING VESSELS OF THE GREAT LAKES

The BOSTON
MILLS PRESS

A Boston Mills Press Book

Photographs and Text copyright © 2014 Greg McDonnell

Second Printing 2023

Library and Archives Canada Cataloguing in Publication

A CIP record for this title is available from Library and Archives Canada

Publisher Cataloging-in-Publication Data (U.S.)

A CIP record for this title is available from Library of Congress

Back cover: Chasing the *Agawa Canyon* up the St. Clair River, Great Lakes Fleet 1000-footer *Edwin H. Gott* follows the Algoma Central self-unloader into the bend at St. Clair, Michigan, on September 3, 2005.

Page 1: Chadburn ship's telegraph, *St. Marys Challenger*, November 2006.

Page 2: Algosteel, upbound at Welland Canal Lock 6, passes *Maritime Trader*, downbound on maiden voyage, October 2005.

Page 3: Maumee, downbound, Straits of Mackinac, Michigan, October 2006.

Page 5: Shore-leave board, *James Norris*

Published by
Boston Mills Press, 2014

In Canada:
Distributed by Firefly Books Ltd.
50 Staples Avenue, Unit 1, Richmond Hill, Ontario
Canada L4B 0A7

In the United States:
Distributed by Firefly Books (U.S.) Inc.
P.O. Box 1338, Ellicott Station, Buffalo, New York
USA 14205

Design: Sue Breen and Chris McCorkindale
McCorkindale Advertising & Design

Printed in China

CONTENTS

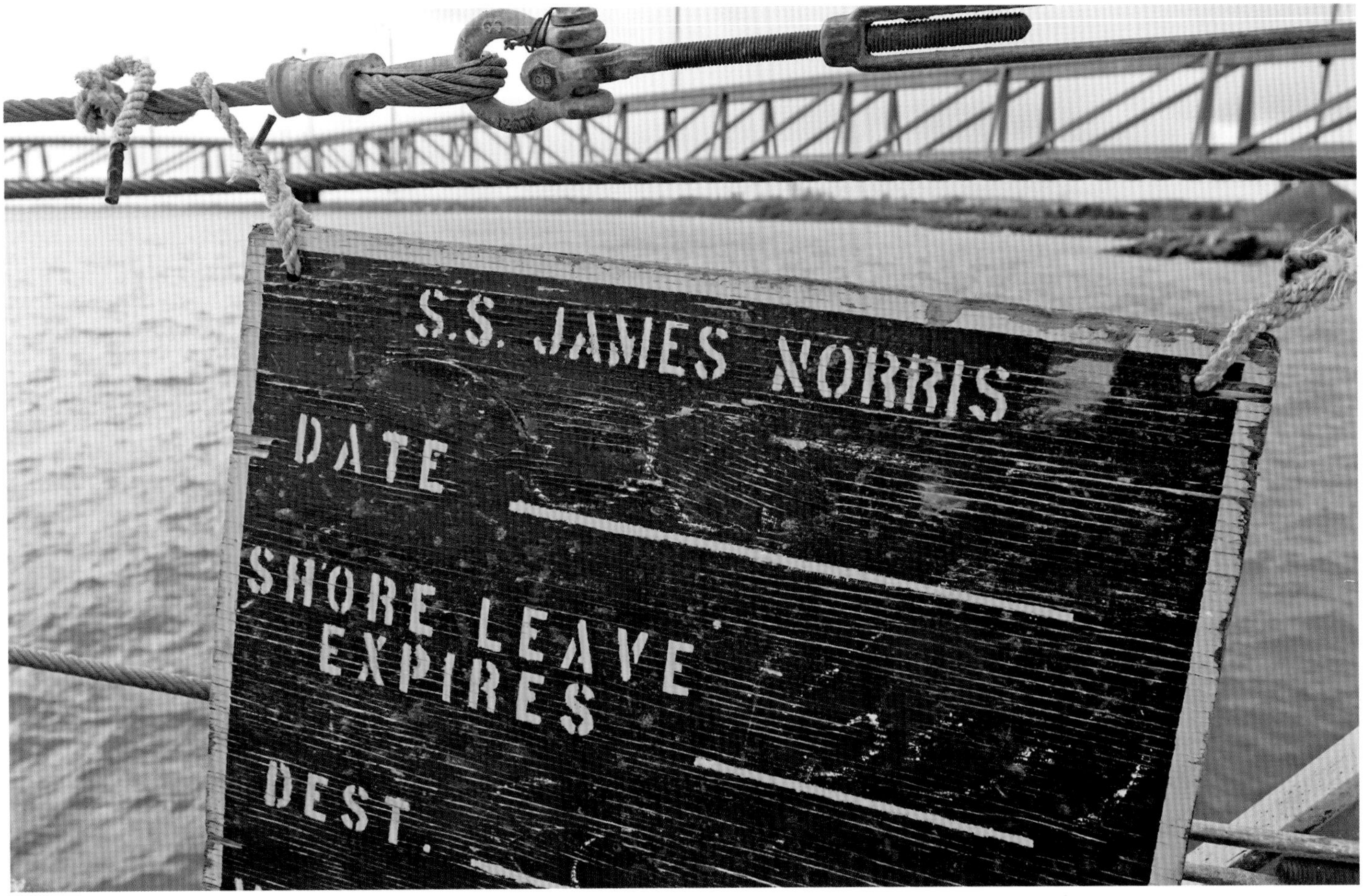
S.S. JAMES NORRIS
DATE
SHORE LEAVE
EXPIRES
DEST.

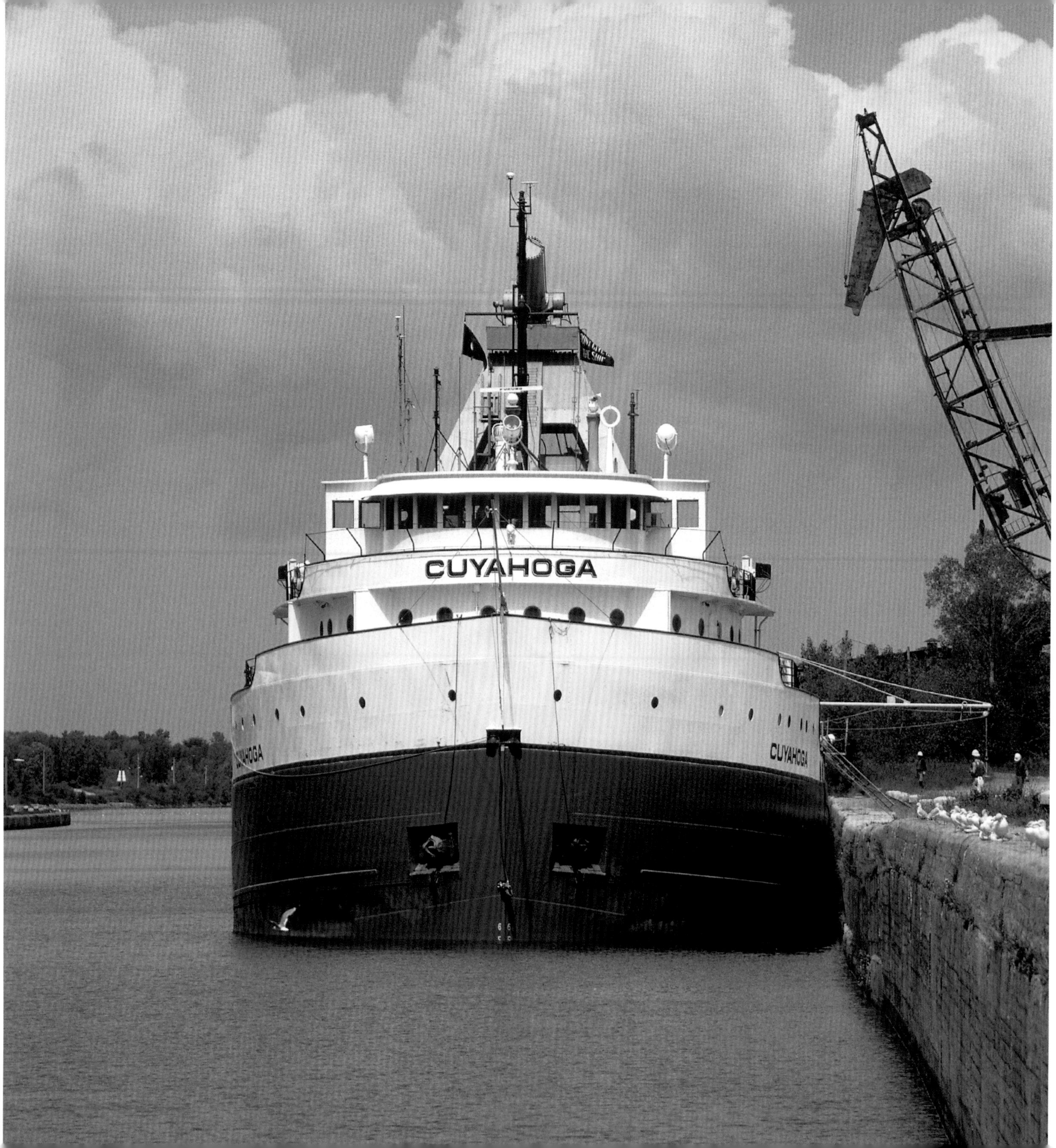
CUYAHOGA
CUYAHOGA

ACKNOWLEDGMENTS

THE STUFF OF DREAMS

Blame it on steam ... steam and Carl Bury, third engineer on Lower Lakes Towing Company's S.S. *Cuyahoga*. It was steam, specifically *Cuyahoga's* rare Lentz Marine Standard engine, that prompted me to seek out the ship at Port Colborne, Ontario, on a hot afternoon in August 1999. It was Carl Bury who arranged permission to board *Cuyahoga* — at the time, one of just four vessels powered by reciprocating steam engines that remained active on the Great Lakes — as she loaded stone on the banks of the Welland Canal. Had it not been for that encounter, this book would not exist.

Until that muggy August day, the closest I'd been to a laker was a brush — quite literally — with an Upper Lakes Shipping straight-decker docked in Hamilton harbor in 1979 as my then wife-to-be, Maureen, a frustrated Russian would-be sailor and I brought our barely under control sailboat alongside the towering freighter as we fumbled through sailing lessons conducted by the Hamilton Harbour Commission. All that changed as I followed Carl Bury down the engine-room stairs for an audience with *Cuyahoga's* great four-crank, double-compound, reciprocating-steam power plant. It was in the steam and sweltering heat of the engine room that the inspiration for this work was born.

Steam was the catalyst, but it was the taste of adventure, sense of history and the introduction to the majesty and mystique of the traditional lake boat — powered by steam, steam turbine or diesel — that inspired this work. These pages are tribute to the enduring vessels of the Great Lakes and to the mariners who serve on them.

Eight years in the making, the creation of this book has allowed me to sail the five Great Lakes and to spend time on a number of vessels, including the 100-year-old steam-powered cement carrier *St. Marys Challenger;* Upper Lakes Shipping self-unloader *James Norris* and straight-decker *Canadian Miner;* Essroc's cement-hauling *Stephen; B. Roman;* Lower Lakes Towing's *Cuyahoga* and *Saginaw;* and the Lake Michigan car ferry *Badger,* the last coal-fired steamer on the Lakes.

There's been time, too, to ride tugs, including the *Ian Mac* as she and sisters *Donald Bert* and *Debbie Lyn* assisted the *John D. Leitch* into the harbor at Goderich, Ontario, in heavy Lake Huron seas. And legendary Detroit River mail boat *J.W. Westcott II* — the only floating United States Post Office and the only boat with its own zip code.

Docked at the foot of 24th Street in Detroit, zip code 48222, the *J.W. Westcott II* delivers mail, food, parts and supplies to passing vessels, and

Ed Dewling, captain, *James Norris.*

Spyros Syros, first mate, *Saginaw*.

Martin Desaulniers, chief engineer, *James Norris*.

Ron Bodos, wheelsman, *Saginaw*.

accepts outgoing shipments in return. The Westcott's unique "mail by the pail" service has been a Detroit River institution since 1874, when founder J.W. Westcott commenced mid-river deliveries using a rowboat.

The experience gained in gathering the images on these pages has been the stuff of dreams: leaning on the rail sipping hot coffee on a cold winter night as *Cuyahoga* churns through the Lake Erie ice; steaming through a thick Lake Superior fog on a damp September midnight as the plaintive call of *Saginaw's* fog whistle bellows through the dark; sailing past the Superior grave of the *Edmund Fitzgerald* and getting chills as veteran mariners on the bridge speak in hushed tones of that unforgettable night; sailing proudly

into Milwaukee aboard the *St. Marys Challenger* on a rainy November evening and standing out on the deck as the century-old steamer carefully inches past the old C&NW Kinnickinnic River swing-bridge; probing the oily innards of a Vickers-Skinner Unaflow steam engine with *James Norris* Chief engineer Martin Desaulniers ... hours spent in wheelhouses, in engine rooms and galleys; nights in wood-paneled staterooms ... a week sampling the wares of *Saginaw* cook Randy Landry, purveyor of arguably the finest fare on the Lakes.

None of this would have been possible without the invaluable assistance of a number of people. I am deeply indebted to Scott Bravener of Lower Lakes Towing, John Greenway and Cathy Hoadley

of Seaway Maritime Transport, Edward Hogan and Aaron Bensinger of Hannah Marine; to captains James R. Scott, Hugh Pink, Ed Dewling, George Herdina, Ken Lichtle, Jim Hornblower, and the hard-working, hospitable crews of ships that have welcomed me aboard.

These pages are enriched by the contributions of friends and talented photographers who have generously shared their work: Michael Valentine, Jeff Mast, Mike Harting, Jim Koglin and Brad Jolliffe, who accompanied me, not only on that initial visit aboard the *Cuyahoga*, but on a number of subsequent voyages.

If not for the encouragement and support of my wife and best friend, Maureen, this work would be little more than a dream.

Above left: George Herdina, captain, *St. Marys Challenger*. Above middle: Hugh Pink, captain, *Saginaw*. Above right: Greg Courtney, wheelsman, *Saginaw*. Right: Paul Morris, second mate, *James Norris*.

Randy Landry, cook , *Saginaw*.　　　　Jim Hornblower, captain, *Ian Mac*.　　　　Bill Kishel, third mate, *St. Marys Challenger*.

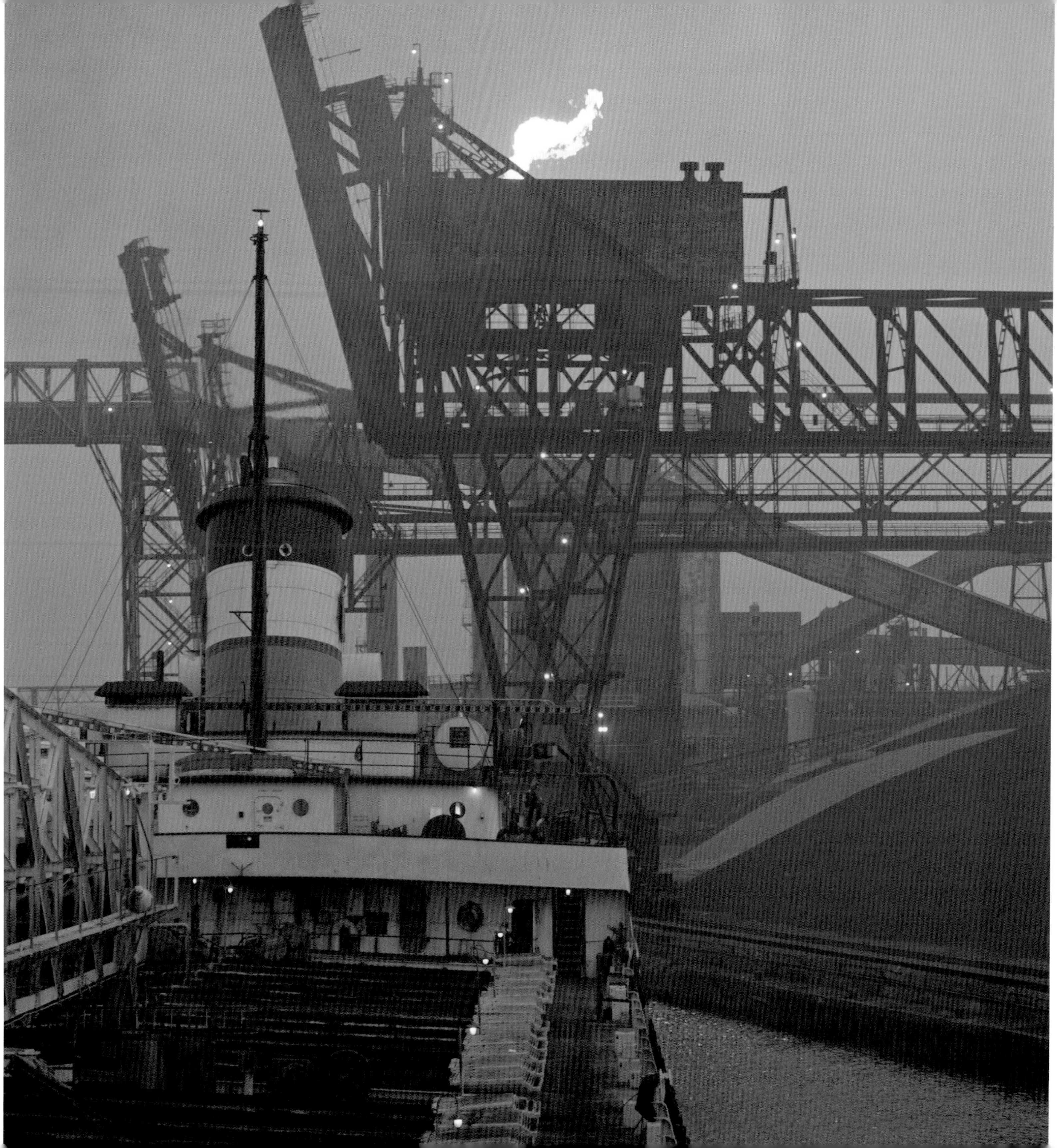

STAIRWAY TO HELL

They call it "the tunnel," the dank, dark corridor running beneath the holds of the S.S. *Saginaw*. It's the underbelly of the ship, the intestine of a self-unloader, where the holds empty their contents onto the conveyors of the self-unloading system.

The atmosphere is hot, humid and heavy with the peat-like aroma of damp coal. It's populated by a small band of "tunnelmen," among the hardest-working members of the *Saginaw* crew. On the best of days, the tunnel is a tough place to work; on the worst of days, it's an unimaginable hell.

On the night of September 11, 2005, as the *Saginaw* crew worked to unload 16,997 tons of "Toledo" and "Sandusky" coal at Algoma Steel, the sign above the doorway to the tunnel — altered with the addition of two pencilled words — says it best: STAIRWAY to hell.

All afternoon, as we sailed up the St. Mary's River toward the Soo, the deckhands and tunnelmen cursed Sandusky coal. It can hang up in the holds, clog the belt and turn an 8-hour unloading job into an 18-to-20-hour nightmare.

The captain was more optimistic. "Toledo coal," he said, "you can set your watch by it. We'll be done in 8 hours."

"The Tunnel," *Saginaw*, Algoma Steel, Sault Ste. Marie, Ontario, September 2005.

The ship was secured at the Algoma Steel dock in Sault Ste. Marie, Ontario, at 17:55. The first coal started running at 18:14. At 20:00, it seemed that the captain just might be right. Minutes later, the self-unloader machinery let out an ungodly racket and the ship fell quiet.

Tension filled the night air. There was trouble below.

Word spread quickly through the ship. The crew's worst fear had come to pass: a gritty mess of coal had clogged the unloader and overburdened the conveyors. Drawn by the suspense, I set out to

Both: Ron Bodos clearing coal from the belt, *Saginaw*, Algoma Steel, Sault Ste. Marie, Ontario, September 2005.

investigate and stepped into the netherworld beyond the heavy steel door marked "Stairway to hell."

Strains of Jimmy Dean's "Big John" filled my head as I descended the stairs into "the dust and smoke of this man-made hell," where men soaked in sweat and coated in coal dust shoveled their way through the tons of black grit clogging the belt. The *Saginaw* crew are no ordinary men. There's a brotherhood about those assigned to the half-century-old steamer. When there's work to be done

—even the dirtiest of work—all hands pitch in, no matter what their formal job description.

The first face I recognized on the belt was that of wheelsman Ron Bodos. "I'll be 70 in eight years," he says. "This is the last job I'll have." Sleeves torn from his Lower Lakes coveralls, beads of sweat glistening in the light of a single bulb overhead, he swings the shovel with abandon.

Big John
Big Bad John

Slugging it out behind Bodos is Syros Spyros, retired from Upper Lakes and working as first mate on the *Saginaw*. Behind Syros, tunnelmen and deckhands labor in the dim light. No one on this ship is afraid of work.

In the dank confines of the tunnel at the bottom of that old ship, I found the spirit and essence of this work. This book is concerned with the venerable ships of the Great Lakes, but it is dedicated to the generations of mariners who have sailed the inland seas and to those who uphold the tradition.

Coal and sweat in the netherworld behind the heavy steel door marked "Stairway to hell," *Saginaw*, Algoma Steel, Sault Ste. Marie, Ontario, September 2005.

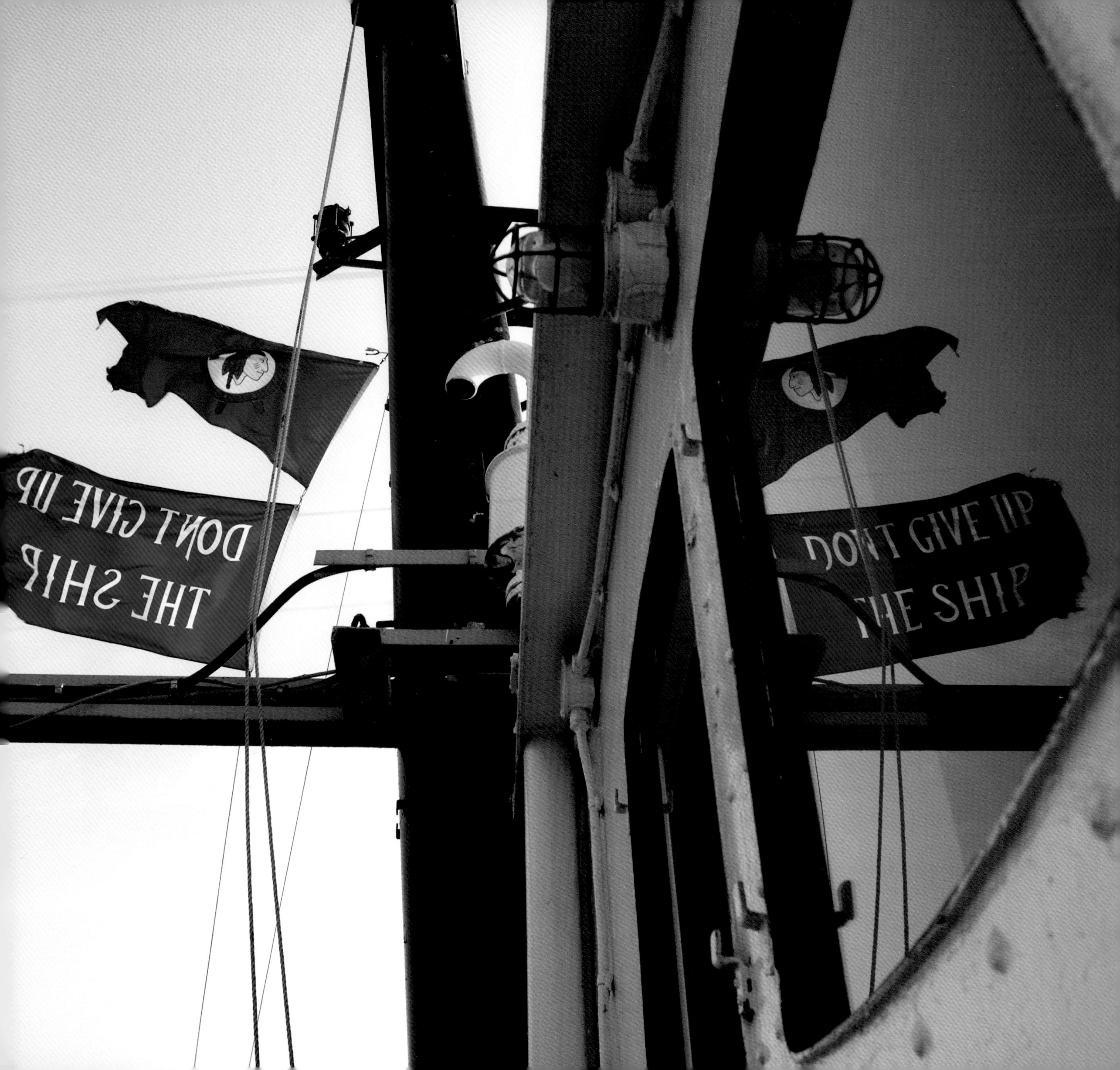
DONT GIVE UP
THE SHIP

DON'T GIVE UP THE SHIP

Don't give up the ship. A simple blue flag emblazoned with the legendary last command uttered by Captain James Lawrence of the U.S.S. *Chesapeake* in 1813 snaps defiantly in the wind as a driving December gale threatens to rip it from the mast of the gray-hulled steamer grinding through the Lake Erie ice. Burdened with some 14,000 tons of Manitoulin Island limestone, S.S. *Cuyahoga*, the 620-foot flagship of the Lower Lakes Towing Co., has battled blizzards, gale-force winds and 20-foot seas to reach Cleveland on a snowy morning two days after Christmas 1999.

Ice clinging to her riveted hull, snow swirling about her decks and hatch covers, steam whispering from deck winches and billowing from her stack, *Cuyahoga* sails victoriously past the pier lights and into the icy black waters of her namesake river. With a spine-tingling blast of her baritone whistle, the big ship announces her arrival as she ducks beneath the Norfolk Southern lift-bridge.

Possessed of classic laker lines, her bow dominated by a grand, curve-faced pilothouse, her stern punctuated by an after house topped with a fat stack resplendent in Lower Lakes' colors and adorned with the company's Indianhead herald, *Cuyahoga* is a sight to behold. Her handsome

Cuyahoga unloading stone, Cleveland, Ohio, December 1999.

dress of Lower Lakes gray and white, with neat red and black trim, accents the sculptured steelwork of her upper decks, the port holes that dot her hull and the subtle beauty of a shipbuilding art that has been lost to time and bottom-line economics. She is the classic laker, the consummate union of function and form.

Tracing its origin to the wooden-hulled *R.J. Hackett* of 1869, the traditional laker is of unique design specific to the Great Lakes. Its cargo holds are bracketed by a pilothouse at the fore and an after house — with crew accommodations, galley and engine room — at the stern. For better than a century, they've been the backbone of Great

---

Left: Don't Give Up the Ship; Lower Lakes house flags, *Saginaw*, September 2005.

15

Engine detail, Lentz Marine Standard reciprocating steam engine, *Cuyahoga*.

Lakes shipping, transporting bulk commodities of iron ore and coal, grain, stone, salt and cement over the inland seas and the St. Lawrence River.

Developed in the early 1900s, but uncommon on larger vessels until the 1950s, self-unloading equipment radicalized lake boat design. Outfitted with a system of belts and conveyors running beneath their holds, self-unloaders are able to discharge their cargo onto belts that feed a deck-mounted unloading boom that can be swung ashore on the port or starboard side. Newer vessels have been constructed as self-unloaders and dozens of older straight-deckers have been modified with the addition of self-unloading equipment.

Purists may balk at the aesthetics of the massive boom and bulky superstructure of the self-unloading equipment shouldered by otherwise handsome ships. However, this concession to modernism is in no small measure responsible for their survival long after so many contemporaries have fallen under the ship-breaker's hammer. While only a handful of unaltered straight-deckers remain in service, self-unloader conversions have

proven to be the salvation of dozens of older bulk carriers still working the lakes.

The last American-flagged straight-decker to be constructed, the sleek-styled 730-foot *Edward L. Ryerson* — built to carry ore for Inland Steel of Chicago — was launched by Manitowoc Ship-building at Manitowoc, Wisconsin, on January 21, 1960. On December 12, 1968, Hall Shipping's *Ottercliffe Hall*, the last conventional straight-deck-er to be built, was launched from Port Weller Dry Docks in St. Catharines, Ontario. Algoma Central Marine self-unloader *Algosoo*, christened at Collingwood Shipyards in Collingwood, Ontario, on November 26, 1974, closed the book on construction of ships of the traditional laker style. The fate of conventional lakers had already been sealed as Bethlehem Steel's 1,000-foot self-unloader *Stewart J. Cort* made her maiden voyage several months earlier, on May 2, 1974.

Unable to fit through the Welland Canal, the 1,000-footers are restricted to Lake Erie and above. That, and the dwindling fortunes of the Great Lakes trade, has limited construction of 1,000-footers to just 13 vessels. None have been built since 1981 when Interlake Steamship's 1,013-foot *William J. Delancy* — the largest vessel on the lakes — was completed by American Ship Building at Lorain, Ohio. Nonetheless, the 1,000-footers have taken their toll on conventional lakers.

Once, they ruled supreme, but the ranks of traditional lake boats have been diminished by age and attrition, by harsh economics and the incursion of "salties," saltwater vessels from overseas. Victims of declining trade, foreign competition and the advent of monstrous 1,000-footers, hundreds of lakers have been sent to scrap over the past few decades. Those that survive are worthy of attention, if not admiration.

Cuyahoga's heavy steel hull-plates bear dents and scars that are testament to more than a half-century of transporting coal, ore and stone on the lakes — and tribute to the muscle and sweat

invested by the workers of the American Ship Building Co., who riveted together Hull No. 828 in the Lorain, Ohio, shipyards in 1943. She's a war baby, one of 16 "Maritimer" class bulk freighters ordered by the United States Maritime Commission for Great Lakes service in World War II. One of six Maritimers designated L6-S-A1, she was christened the *J. Burton Ayers* and made her maiden voyage on August 19, 1943, steaming under the flag of the Cleveland-based Great Lakes Steamship Co., to load iron ore at Duluth, Minnesota. She earned her keep hauling coal and ore to feed the furnaces of steel mills on the lower lakes.

The *J. Burton Ayers* retained her name through a series of ownerships. In 1957, Northwestern Mutual Life Insurance Co. of Milwaukee, Wisconsin, took title to the Ayers, assigning her to a 15-year charter to be operated by Cleveland-based Wilson Marine Transit Co. as part of its takeover of Great Lakes Steamship. Wilson purchased the Ayers outright in 1966. Kinsman Marine Transport acquired the vessel in 1972 and dealt her to the Columbia Transportation Division of Oglebay Norton in 1974. In the process, she was converted to a self-unloader in the Toledo yards of the American Ship Building Company.

Carrying the Columbia star on her stack, the *J. Burton Ayers* plied the lakes until she put into Toledo for winter lay-up in December 1990. For nearly five years, she lay rusting in the Frog Pond on Toledo's industrial waterfront, in a deep hibernation from which even the most optimistic observers wagered she'd never awaken. But for Scott Bravener and his fledgling Lower Lakes Towing Co., of Port Dover, Ontario, the tale of Hull No. 828 might well have ended there in the muddy backwaters of the Frog Pond.

"She was written up for scrap when we got her," says Captain James R. Scott over coffee in the wheelhouse of his 620-foot charge. Lower Lakes purchased the decommissioned *J. Burton*

class A1s and built the foundation of what would soon become a proud fleet of reborn lakers. Bearing a new name in honor of her Cleveland roots and the river that would again be a frequent port of call, *Cuyahoga* set sail carrying the Lower Lakes standard.

Traces of steam hissing from deck winches and drifting from the veteran laker's stack betray the fact that *Cuyahoga* has not given over to the new order. Not yet, at least. Indeed, as she churns slowly up the river with which she shares her name, *Cuyahoga* is propelled by the same reciprocating steam, four-crank, double-compound Lentz Standard marine engine lowered into her hull by the shipbuilders at Lorain. Time, however, is about to catch up with the old steamer. In less than a week, she's scheduled for winter lay-up at Sarnia, where her faithful Lentz steam engine and Combustion Engineering Co. water-tube boilers will be lifted out and replaced with a Caterpillar 3608 diesel. For the moment, though, the giant Lentz engine beats methodically, as if it could run forever.

On a frigid December day, *Cuyahoga's* engine room is an irresistible haven. The sweet aroma of hot oil and steam is intoxicating; the rhythmic motion of massive, frighteningly powerful connecting rods and cranks is mesmerizing. Like most reciprocating steam engines, the Lentz Marine Standard keeps no secrets. Its moving parts, from muscular rods to tiny lubricators, are almost all exposed and, by necessity, accessible.

In the dim glow of caged incandescent lights, connecting rods slathered in lube oil delivered from a simple drip system move lazily up and down. Even at top speed, the Lentz turns at an easy 78 revolutions per minute as third engineer Carl Bury makes his rounds. With a physician's touch, he carefully examines the old Lentz, feeling the temperature of bearings and joints with the back of his hand, watching every move, listening to every beat of the engine.

"Ahead slow." Engine room Chadburn, *Cuyahoga*, Cuyahoga River, Cleveland, Ohio, December 1999. The ancient device has felt the begrimed and calloused hands of generations of engineers. Bury's will be among the last.

Ayers in the summer of 1995 and had her towed to Sarnia, Ontario, for refit. She was dressed in a fresh coat of Lower Lakes gray and white, given formal Canadian registry and christened *Cuyahoga* in November 1995. Bravener breathed new life into the lone survivor of the Maritime

Carl Bury at controls of Lentz Marine Standard engine, *Cuyahoga*, December 1999.

Carl Bury, third engineer, *Cuyahoga*, December 1999.

At the end of his rounds, Bury leans pensively against the polished brass Chadburn ship's telegraph in the engine room. The ancient device, used to communicate engine operating orders from pilothouse to engine room, has felt the be-grimed and calloused hands of generations of engineers. Bury's will be among the last.

Dieselization of the *Cuyahoga* will include conversion to bridge-controlled engine operation, ending the ritual of orders and responses relayed over twinned Chadburns.

"I'll probably move over to the *Saginaw*," muses Bury, referring to *Cuyahoga*'s newly acquired steam turbine-powered fleet mate. "I'll stick with steam," he adds, just before the bell on the Chadburn interrupts the thought.

"Ahead slow!" the Chadburn bell rings out as the inner indicator needle moves to the "ahead slow" position on the dial. Bury ratchets the brass handle into the corresponding position in response and moves instinctively to execute the order at the throttle of the Lentz. Furiously turning the set of large cast-iron wheels that control engine direction and speed, he reins in the big steamer.

For much of the next two hours, the Chadburn will ring like a carillon: half ahead … half astern … half ahead … dead slow ahead … Bury and the Lentz will get a work out as Captain Scott

maneuvers the big ship through impossibly tight bends in the river the Mohawk tribe once called Cayagaga, or "crooked."

In the wheelhouse, Scott surveys the river ahead, calmly directing the wheelsman, managing the bow thruster and telegraphing orders to Bury over the Chadburn. As the snow falls, *Cuyahoga* steams silently past bars and restaurants in the gentrified Flats, past derelict riverfront factories and freight houses, beneath concrete-and-steel viaducts and along twisting railroad spurs. The bow of the ship sweeps within feet of spalled concrete docks like the second hand of a giant clock as Scott guides the 620-foot vessel through the curving course of the *Cuyahoga* with deceptive ease and heart-stopping accuracy.

As *Cuyahoga* closes in on the CBS 2 dock, deck-hands scramble to prepare for arrival: wires are tossed ashore, steam winches chatter as they snug the ship against the dock, hatch covers are opened, the unloading boom swings out, conveyors rumble, holds open, and Manitoulin Island stone hits Ohio soil. The old vessel shudders and shakes as its self-unloading system of belts and conveyors digests than 10,000 tons of limestone, sending it ashore at a rate of better than 3,000 net tons per hour.

Over the low rumble of rock rattling through the ship's innards and the howl of a hard wind pushing at the door, Captain Scott reminisces at the dinner table. There's time for tales of years at the helm of Algoma Central ships, of a battle of wills and showdown of skills with a Chicago River tug, of life on the lakes and changing times. Scott has words of praise for his crew, and for the aging ship that is his current command. "This one's the last of the Mohicans … the one with all the character."

By nightfall, *Cuyahoga*'s holds are empty and a stern line is stretched to the "G tug" *Idaho*, which stands ready to assist on the return down-river. While bow-thrusters make it practical for skilled mariners to pilot vessels upstream

Securing the hatches, *Cuyahoga*, Cleveland, Ohio, December 1999.

Cuyahoga making turn in Cuyahoga River, Cleveland, Ohio, December 1999.

unassisted, the lack of a turning basin near the stone dock makes it necessary for *Cuyahoga* to reverse downstream … a difficult move best made with the help of a tug.

At 18:38, First Mate Mike Kilpatrick gives a single blast of the whistle. The shore lines are cast off, chugging steam winches draw in the wires, and deckhands work to secure the hatches. Two minutes later, the *Idaho* and *Cuyahoga* exchange whistle signals and get under way as the little tug heaves mightily on the line linking the vessels.

In *Cuyahoga*'s darkened pilothouse, the captain, mate and wheelsman concentrate on the delicate business at hand. There's no room for error or misjudgment. The mate counts down distances relayed from the deck, "75 off the knuckle… midship…55 off the knuckle…"

Shepherding the big ship downstream, the tug *Idaho* seems to be everywhere: off the starboard, then off the port, then straight ahead. The mastery of its movement is magnificent as the tethered vessels trace the twisting course of the Cuyahoga River in perfect synchronization at a steady two knots.

Terminal Tower and the lights of Cleveland's Tower City loom overhead and reflect on the water in shimmering shades of red, white and green as *Cuyahoga* makes a graceful turn. The haunting call of a distant whistle echoes through the canyons of concrete and steel as American Steamship Company's *American Republic* chases the *Cuyahoga* all the way down the river.

After a 95-minute downriver ride, the *Idaho* lets go at 20:15. Ten minutes later, *Cuyahoga* is back on Lake Erie with her engine steaming full ahead and her course set for Windsor, Ontario. *American Republic*, bound for Lorain, follows her out into the lake.

A bone-chilling wind whips across the deck as the lights of Cleveland dissolve into the blackest of nights. A wiser man might take to the comfort of his warm cabin on the forecastle deck. I opt instead for wind, freezing spray and a 600-foot stroll … aft to the galley, for a cup of the finest coffee and a handful of homemade cookies. Sleep can wait. This is the time to savour the experience of a steamboat sailing the great inland seas on a stormy winter night.

Steam — generated by the same boilers feeding the cylinders of the Lentz engine urging *Cuyahoga* through the freezing night — warms the forecastle cabin and takes off the chill within minutes. Sleep, however, is another matter. There's drama in the air, in the thundering of the bow slamming the water on the down-stroke of moderate swells, and later, in the hollow banging as the ship grinds through mile after mile of thickening ice.

The jarring ring of the wall-mounted phone above the bed puts an end to any thoughts of sleep. "We're coming up to the River Light," says the voice on the other end. An early wake-up call to join Mike Kilpatrick on the bridge for the journey up the Detroit River seemed like a good idea at midnight. At 03:40, it's lost much of its luster.

Mike Kilpatrick, first mate, *Cuyahoga*, upbound on Lake Erie, December 1999.

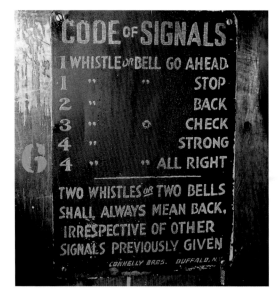

Detail, Lentz Marine Standard reciprocating steam engine, *Cuyahoga*.

Throttle detail, Lentz Marine Standard reciprocating steam engine, *Cuyahoga*.

Stepping back into the night, a blast of cold air revives the senses and a brisk sprint up the steel staircase to the wheelhouse gets the blood flowing. Mike pours freshly brewed coffee; with the first sip, the world is right.

The wheelhouse is dark, illuminated only by the soft glow of the radar screen. Mike and the wheelsman speak in low tones as a Tragically Hip song plays quietly on the radio propped against the window. The marine radio broadcasts word of gale warnings and the conversations of ships passing in the night.

As *Cuyahoga* churns through the ice on the approach to the Detroit River Light, Kilpatrick probes the darkness with a hand-directed spotlight. A tracer beam slices through the black and fixes on the buoys marking the entrance to the river. Kilpatrick gives course adjustments to the wheelsman. Windsor is still two hours distant.

The Chadburn is set at full ahead, as it's been since *Cuyahoga* put Cleveland behind her nearly eight hours earlier. At the other end of the telegraph line that stretches from the bridge to the engine room, the steadfast Lentz Marine Standard works at full steam — unfaltering, unfailing, as it has for most of its 56 years. However, the venerable engine is on borrowed time. Every beat of its cylinders, every turn of its cranks, pushes *Cuyahoga* closer to Windsor and the final trip of the season. One short-turn with a load of salt from Windsor to Toledo and *Cuyahoga* will head for Sarnia and winter lay-up.

Within days, the Lentz will draw its last breath of steam and the great boilers will go permanently cold. For *Cuyahoga*, it will be the end of an era … but it will not be the end. When winter's ice melts from the lakes and the shipping season resumes, she'll set sail from Sarnia with a transplanted Caterpillar diesel beating in her hull. With a new lease on life, she'll rejoin the enduring fleet of traditional lakers engaged in the trade for which they were built, moving ore and coal and rock and grain over the largest freshwater system on Earth.

Against the odds, a stalwart fleet of conventional lakers — straight-deckers, self-unloaders and cement carriers — still rule the Great Lakes. From the *St. Marys Challenger*, launched from the Ecorse, Michigan, yards of Great Lakes Engineering Works in 1907, to the Maritimers — *Cuyahoga* and her L6-S-B1 sisters *Mississagi*, and *Manistee* — of the Second World War, to the *Algosoo*, the last of the traditional lakers, they're the pride of the inland seas.

Working freshwater routes from the Lakehead terminals of Thunder Bay, Duluth and Superior to distant Gulf of St. Lawrence ports of Port Cartier and Sept Iles, they're flagged by U.S. and Canadian concerns, storied Great Lakes companies such as Algoma Central, Upper Lakes, American Steamship, Interlake Steamship and Great Lakes Fleet, to energetic upstarts like Lower Lakes and Voyageur Marine Transport. Steeped in history, distinctive in design and seemingly oblivious to age, the venerable lake boats carry on Great Lakes traditions and trade that date to the nineteenth-century days of wooden ships and iron men. The adopted motto of Scott Bravener's Lower Lakes fleet serves as anthem for all: Don't give up the ship.

Canadian Venture overtakes *Cuyahoga* loading stone, Port Colborne, Ontario, October 2000.

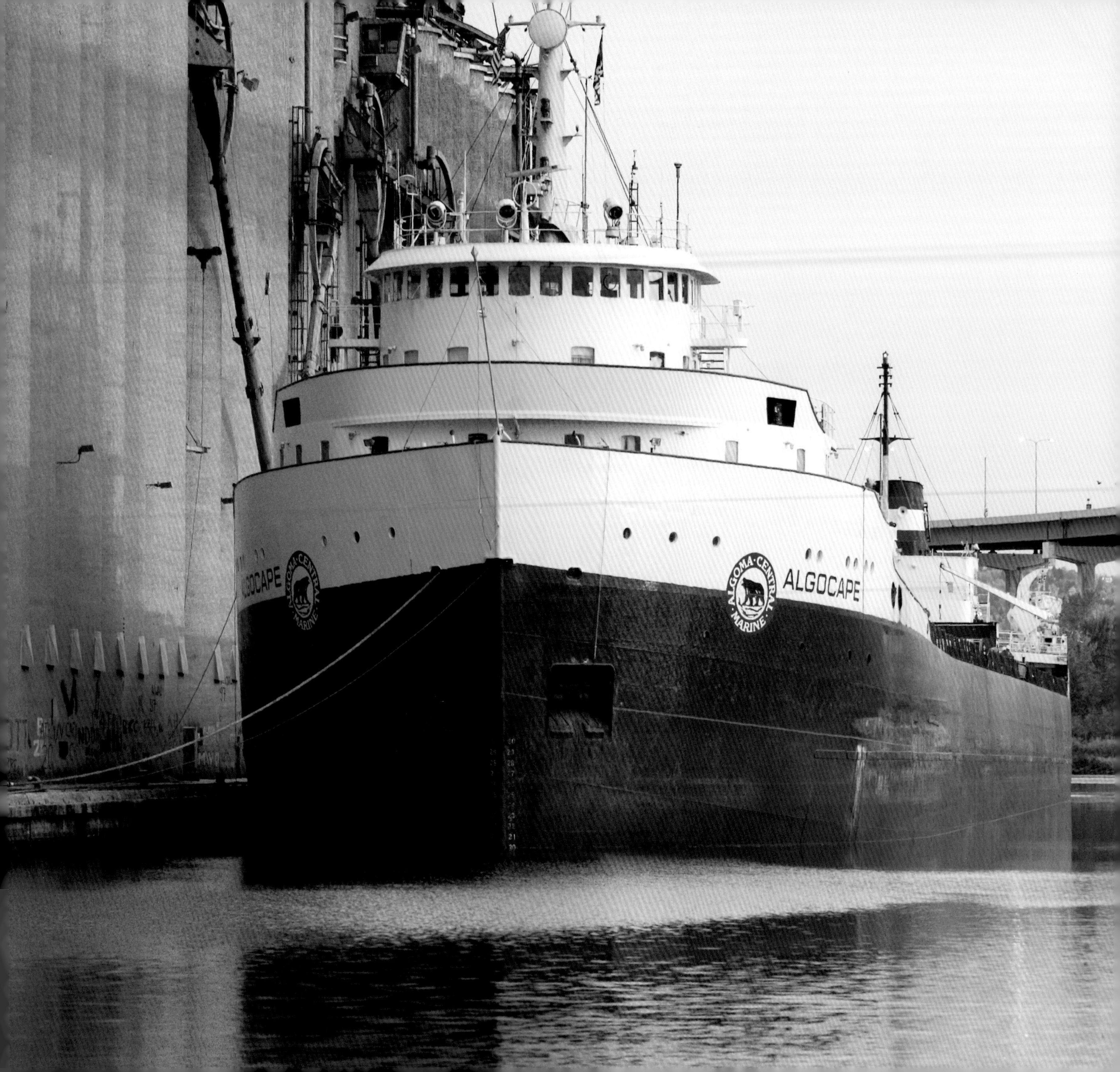
ALGOCAPE
ALGOMA CENTRAL MARINE

Saginaw loading grain, JRI elevator, Thunder Bay, Ontario, September 2005.

Left: *Algocape* loading grain at CHS elevator,
Superior, Wisconsin, October 2006.

Canadian Provider downbound on St. Clair River, Marysville, Michigan, September 2006.

Canadian Voyager upbound on Welland Canal at Thorold, Ontario, August 2001.

Seaway Queen and
Canadian Trader in lay-up,
Toronto, Ontario,
October 2000.

Michipicoten approaching Burlington Piers, Burlington, Ontario, October 2004.

Reserve downbound on the St. Mary's River at Three Mile, Michigan.

MIKE HARTING

Montrealais inbound at Burlington, Ontario, with Port Cartier ore for Dofasco, November 2005.

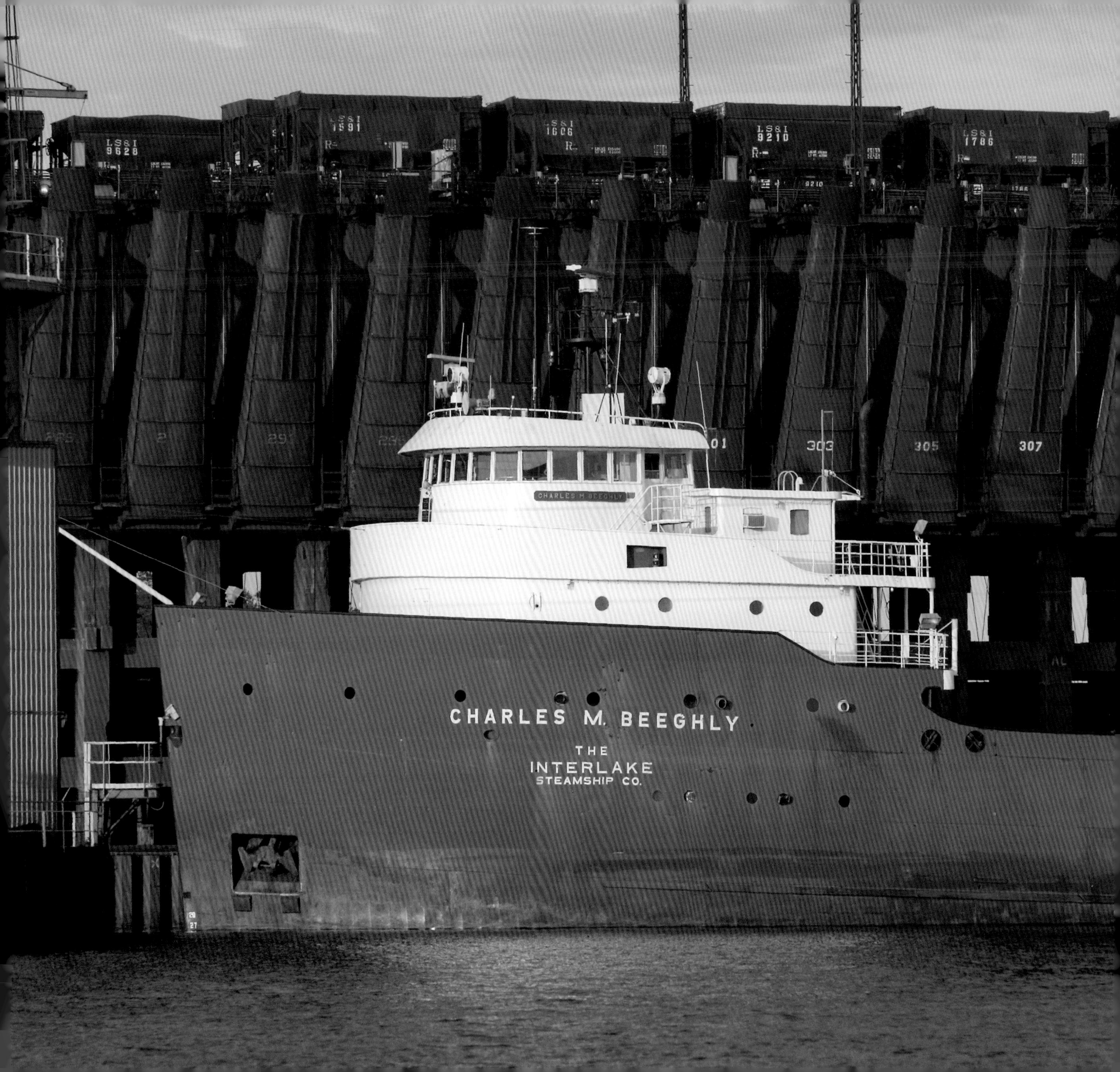
LS&I 9628
LS&I 1591
LS&I 1606
LS&I 9210
LS&I 1786
303
305
307
CHARLES M BEEGHLY
CHARLES M. BEEGHLY
THE
INTERLAKE
STEAMSHIP CO.

Charles M. Beeghly departing Marquette, Michigan, August 2006.

Left: *Charles M. Beeghly*, Lake Superior & Ishpeming ore dock,
Marquette, Michigan, August 2006.

Alpena arriving from Milwaukee, Waukegan, Illinois, March 2006.

She's steam. *Alpena*,
March 2006.

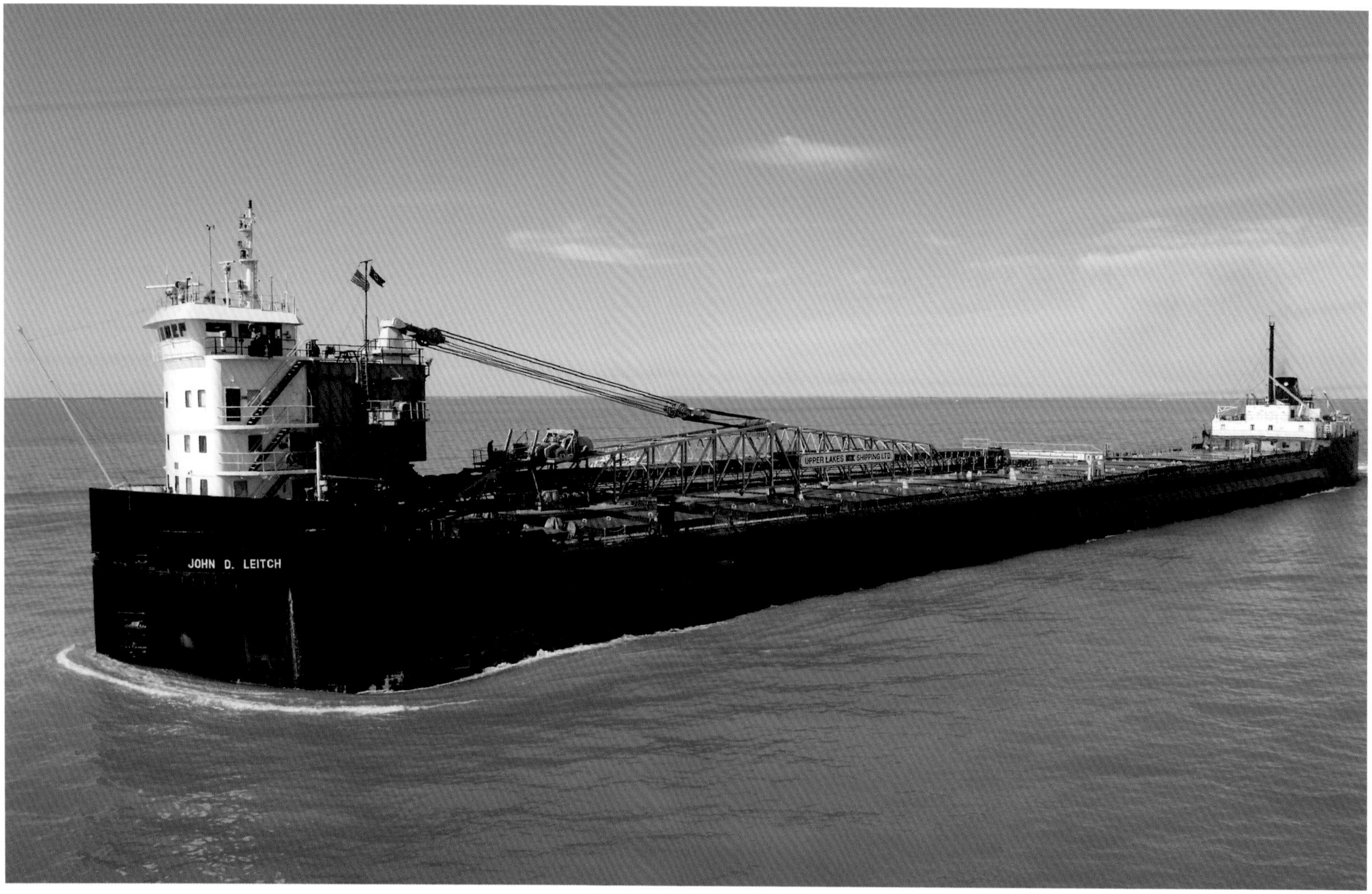
JOHN D. LEITCH
UPPER LAKES SHIPPING LTD.

John D. Leitch downbound on St. Clair River, St. Clair Crib Light, Michigan, September 2005.

Tugs *Ian Mac, Donald Bert*
and *Debbie Lyn* assisting
John D. Leitch at
Goderich, Ontario,
September 2005.

37

Frontenac approaching Burlington, Ontario, bound for Hamilton with iron ore.

Kaye E. Barker outbound on Rouge River, Detroit, Michigan, July 2006.

Halifax on Rouge River, Detroit, Michigan, May 2001.

Detail, Canada Steamship Lines lettering on *Niagara*, Port Colborne, Ontario, October 2000.

James Norris, St. Lawrence Cement, Colborne, Ontario.

James Norris loading limestone, St. Lawrence Cement, Colborne, Ontario.

Mantadoc upbound at Bridge 5, Welland Canal, St. Catharines, Ontario, November 2001.

Former *Mantadoc* downbound exiting Lock 7 in Welland Canal on maiden journey as *Maritime Trader*, October 2005.

Calumet unloading stone River Rouge, Michigan, May 2002.

Stack detail, Lower Lakes Towing *Saginaw*, September 2005.

Courtney Burton unloading grain, General Mills Frontier Elevator, Buffalo, New York, June 2005.

Joseph H. Frantz loading wheat for Huron, Ohio, at Port Stanley, Ontario, August 2004.

BRAD JOLLIFFE

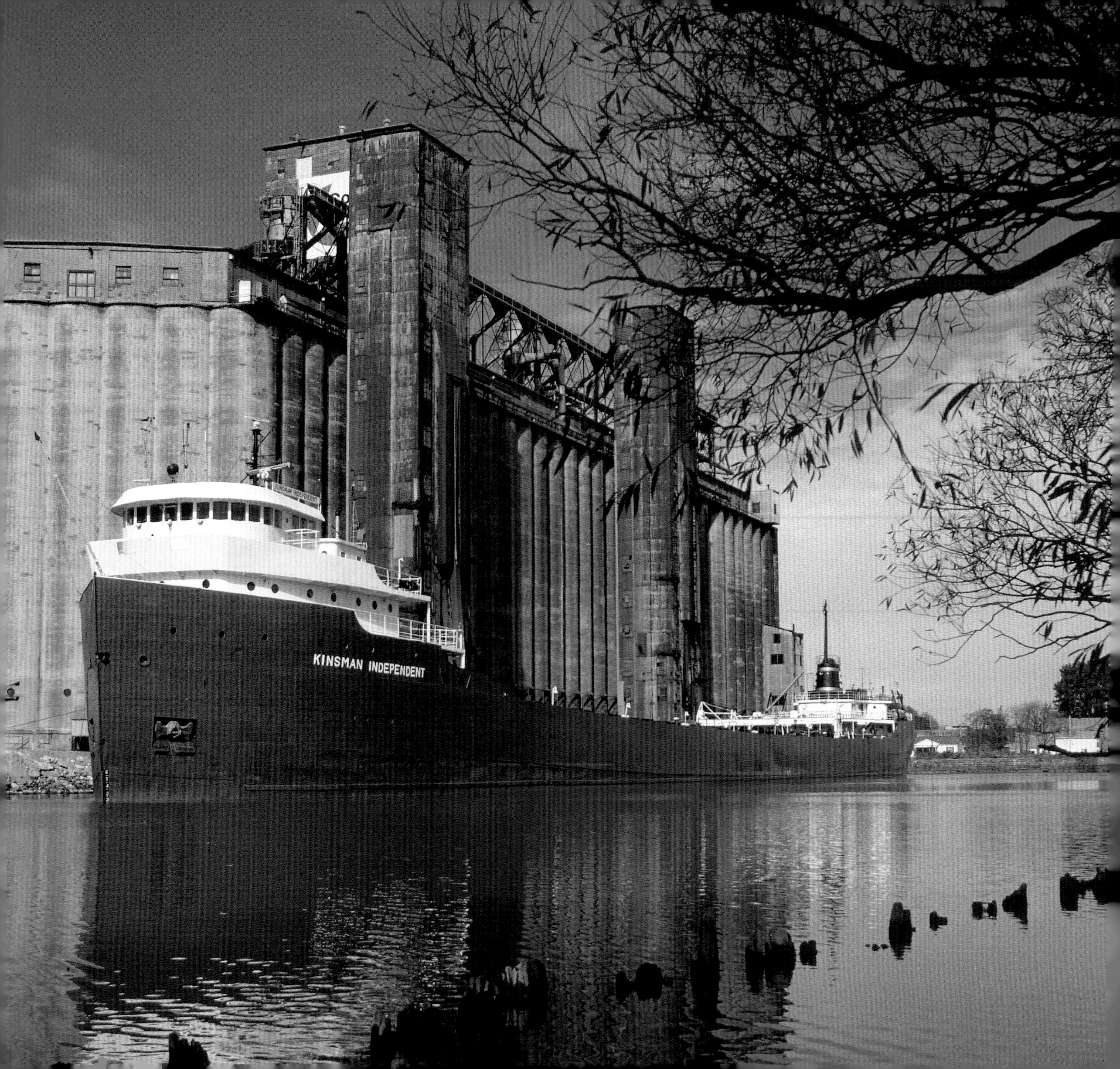
KINSMAN INDEPENDENT

Voyageur Independent — former *Kinsman Independent* — upbound on Detroit River, Detroit, Michigan, November 2005.

Left: *Kinsman Independent,* Conagra elevator,
Buffalo, New York, October 2000.

Detail, Algoma Central *Algosteel*, October 2005.

Agawa Canyon upbound, St. Clair River, St. Clair, Michigan, September 2005.

John D. Leitch below Lock 1, Welland
Canal, St. Catharines, Ontario,
December 2004.

Detail, ice formed on *John D. Leitch*, St. Catharines, Ontario, December 2004.

Algosteel meeting *Halifax* in Welland Canal, Port Robinson, Ontario, May 2002.

Canadian Venture, *Canadian Leader* and *Canadian Mariner* in lay-up, Toronto, Ontario, January 2002.

Cason J. Callaway downbound on the St. Clair River at Sarnia, Ontario, October 2006.

Right: *Canadian Miner* upbound on Lake Superior, 47.02.277N/85.32.880W, September 2005.

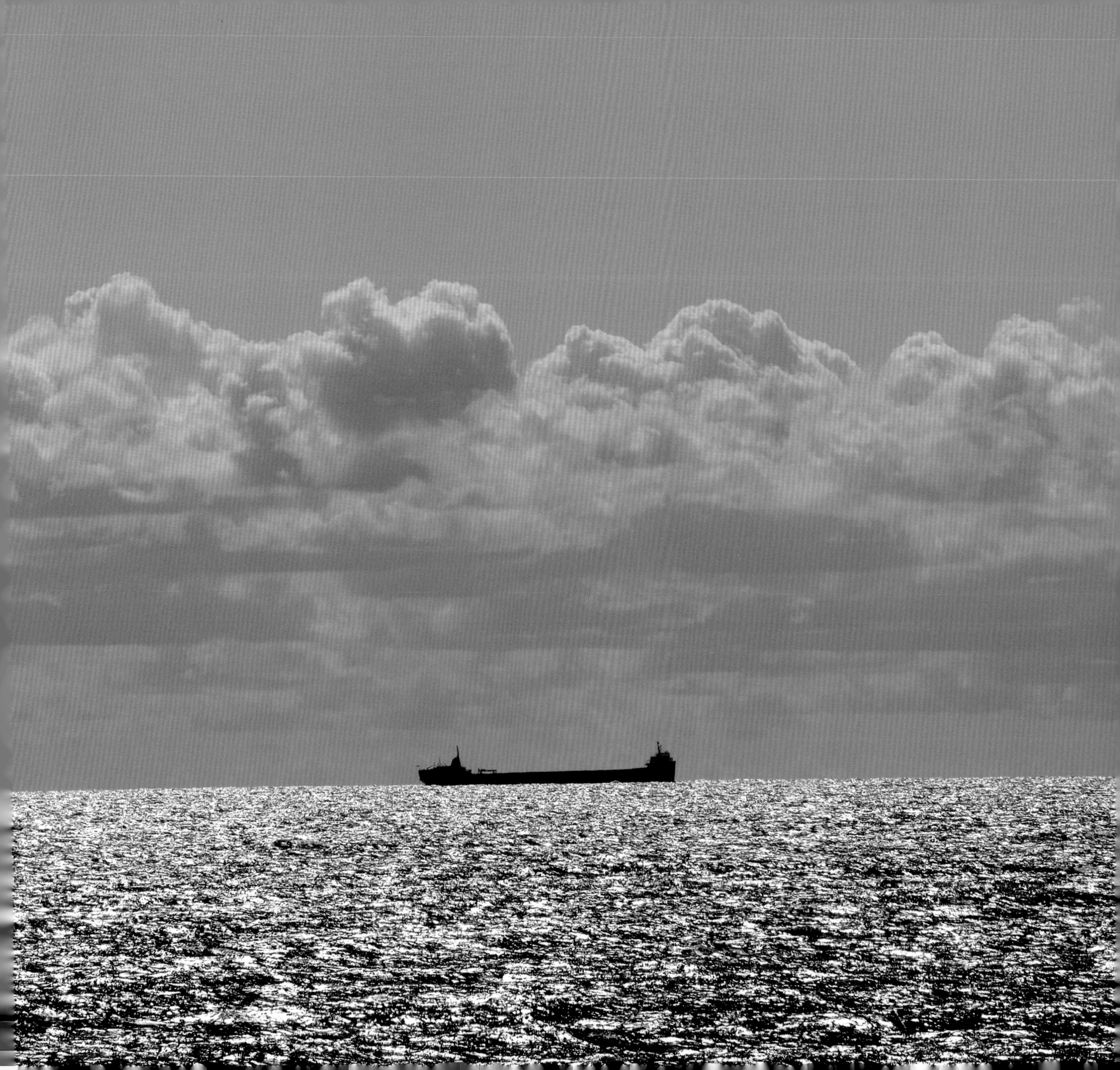

Edward L. Ryerson, Sault Ste. Marie,
Michigan, October 2005.

60

Edward L. Ryerson, St. Mary's River, Sault Ste. Marie, Michigan, October 2005.

Edward L. Ryerson downbound at Sault Ste. Marie, Michigan, with iron ore from Superior to Lorain, Ohio, October 2005.

Edward L. Ryerson framed in stern of *Valley Camp.*

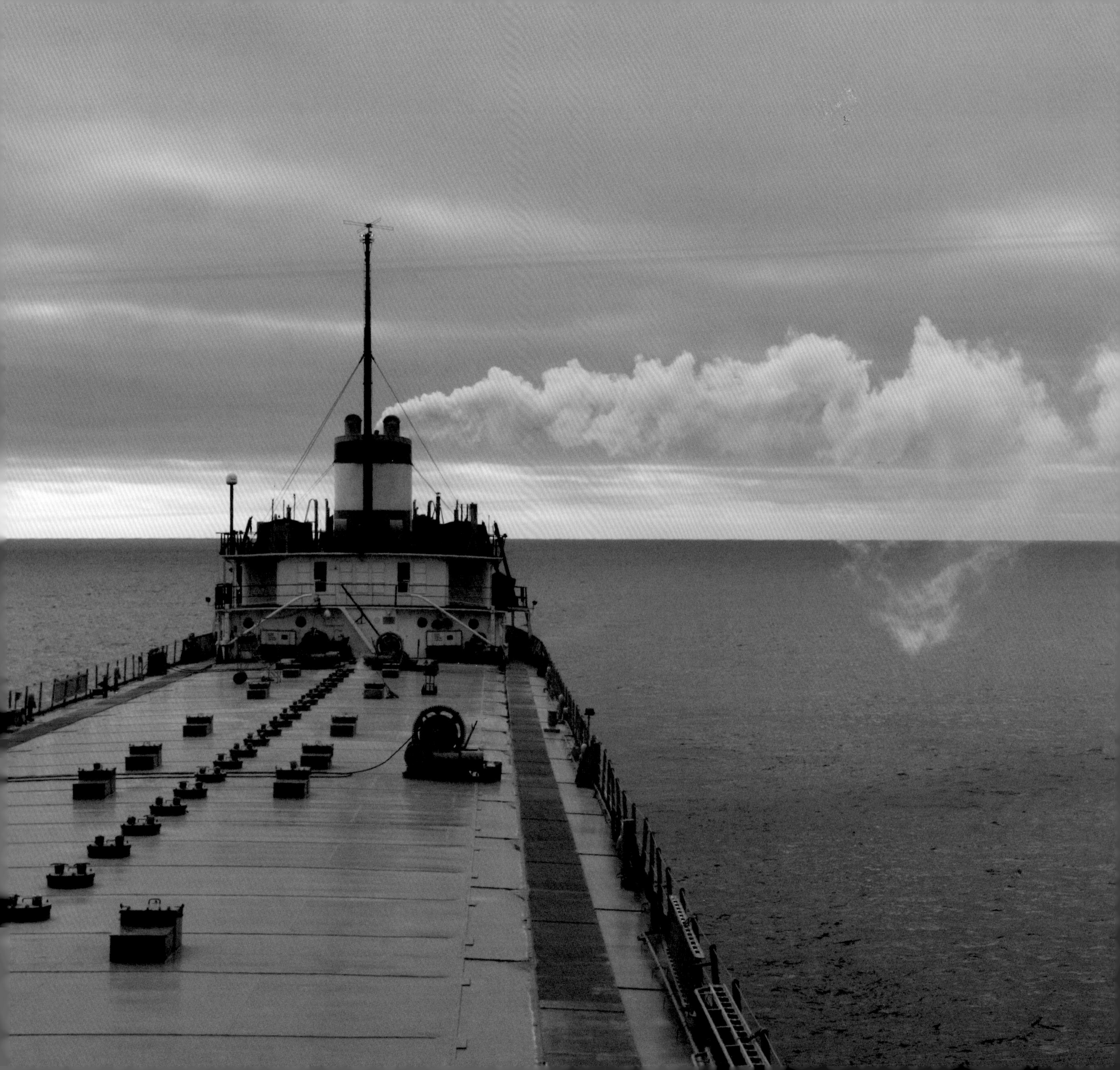

St. Marys Challenger arriving at Grand Haven, Michigan, bound for Ferrysburg, October 2005.

JEFF MAST

Left: Winter morning on Lake Michigan, *St. Marys Challenger*,
November 2006.

Saginaw loading grain, JRI Terminal, Thunder Bay, Ontario, September 2005.

Saginaw, JRI Terminal,
Thunder Bay, Ontario,
September 2005.

Detail, grain spouts loading, *Saginaw*,
JRI Terminal, Thunder Bay, Ontario,
September 2005.

Saginaw loading grain, Mission Terminal, Thunder Bay, Ontario, September 2005.

Algosteel, above Lock 1, Welland Canal, St. Catharines, Ontario, October, 2005.

Maumee downbound on St. Clair River, St. Clair Crib Light, Michigan, September 2005.

Peter Poree, oiler, *St. Marys Challenger,* Milwaukee, Wisconsin, September 2006.

Right: Engine room, *St. Marys Challenger,*
Lake Michigan, November 2006.

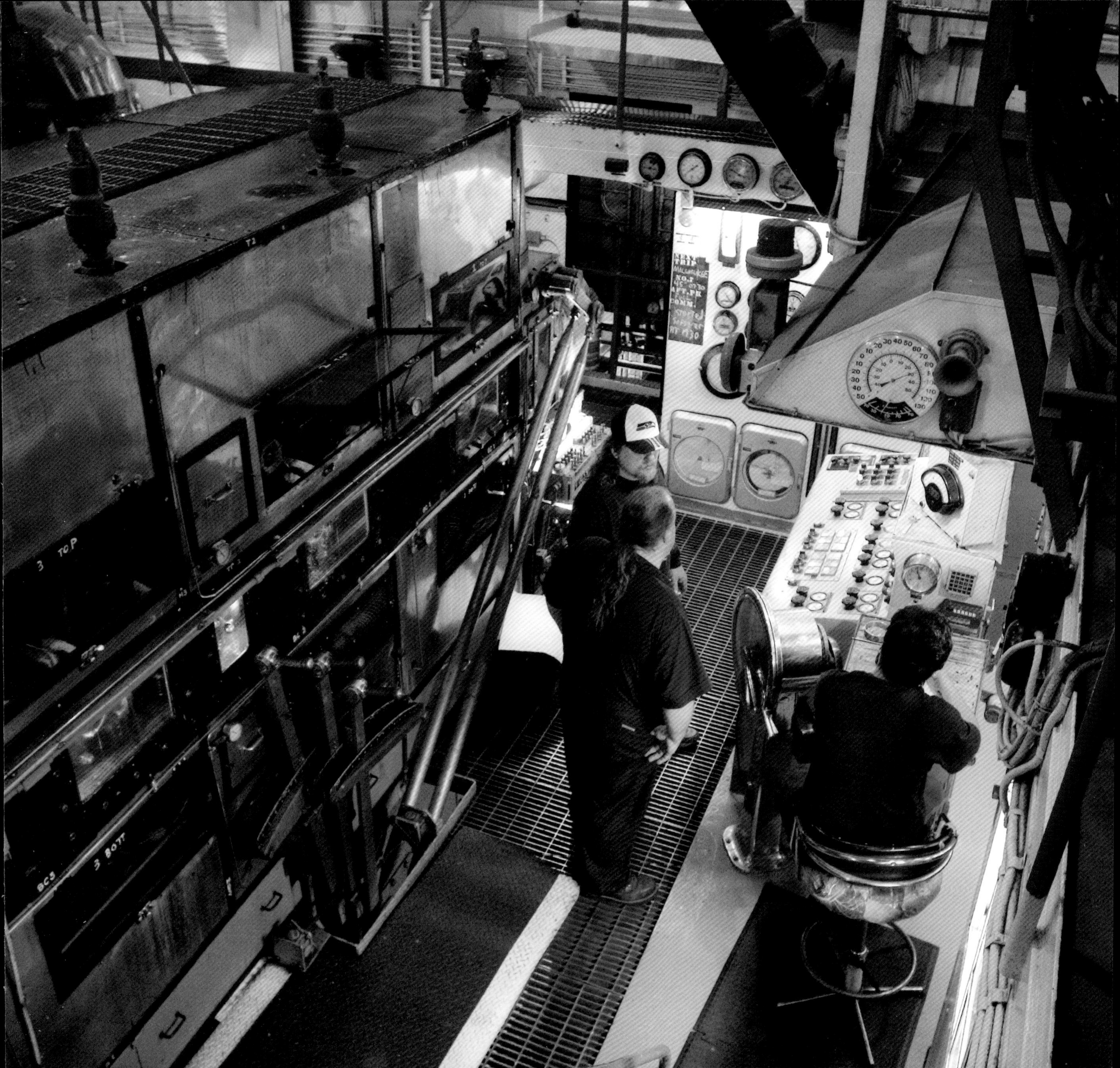
3 TOP
3 BOTT

Oakglen downbound in Welland Canal, Port Robinson, Ontario, July 2000.

BRAD JOLLIFFE

Mapleglen, upbound, meets downbound *Algocape* in Welland Canal, Thorold, Ontario, September 2000.

BRAD JOLLIFFE

Detail, steam deck winch, *James Norris*, October 2006.

St. Marys Challenger, wheelsman operating steam deck winches on departure from Charlevoix, Michigan, November 2006.

Propeller detail, *Canadian Miner*,
Hamilton, Ontario, March 2005.

Detail, *Saginaw,*
Goderich, Ontario,
October 2004.

Canadian Leader with tugs *Glenevis* and *Seahound* above Lock 1, Welland Canal, St. Catharines, Ontario, October 2005.

J.A.W. Iglehart in temporary lay-up, Municipal Dock, Superior, Wisconsin, October 2006.

Arthur M. Anderson loading shale at DM&IR ore dock, Two Harbors, Minnesota, October 2006.

American Victory downbound after mail pickup from *J.W. Westcott II*, Detroit River, Detroit, Michigan, July 2006.

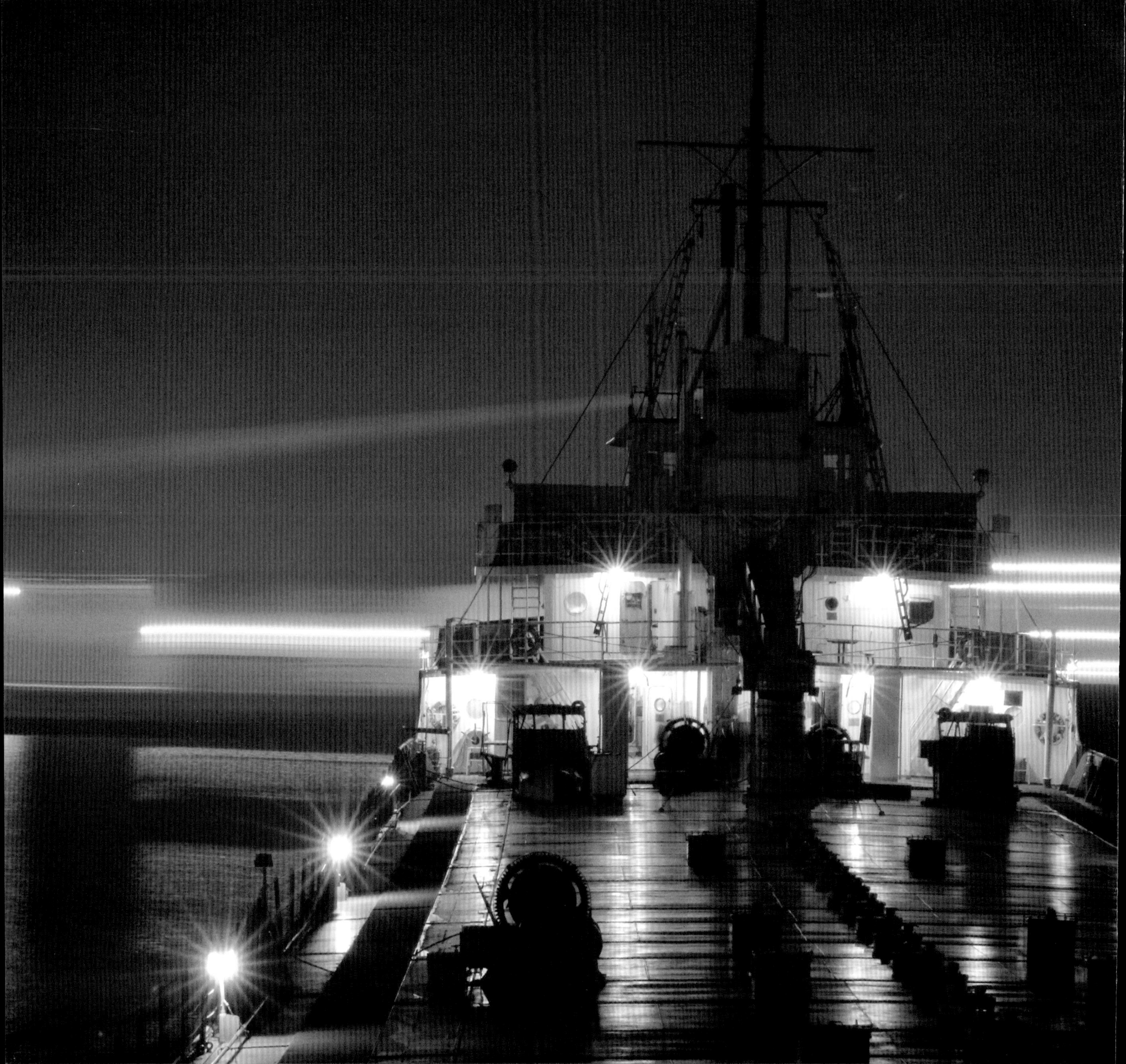

Manistee on Rouge River, Detroit, Michigan, December 2005.

Left: *St. Marys Challenger*, arriving Milwaukee,
Wisconsin, November 2006.

Agawa Canyon, Elton Hoyt 2nd, Algobay and *Desmarais* upbound on Lake Huron at Sarnia, Ontario, April 2000.

Frontenac downbound at Sarnia, Ontario, April 2000.

Algosteel and G Tug *Maine* in Rouge River ice, Detroit, Michigan, April 2005.

Saginaw, Mississagi and *Calumet* in winter lay-up, Sarnia, Ontario, February 2003.

Philip R. Clarke at BNSF Allouez ore dock, Superior, Wisconsin, June 2004.

Myron C. Taylor loading stone,
Welland Canal, Port Colborne,
Ontario, December 1999.
BRAD JOLLIFFE

Alpena unloading at LaFarge Cement, Milwaukee, Wisconsin, March 2006.

Right: Reflection, *Alpena*, Milwaukee, Wisconsin, March 2006.

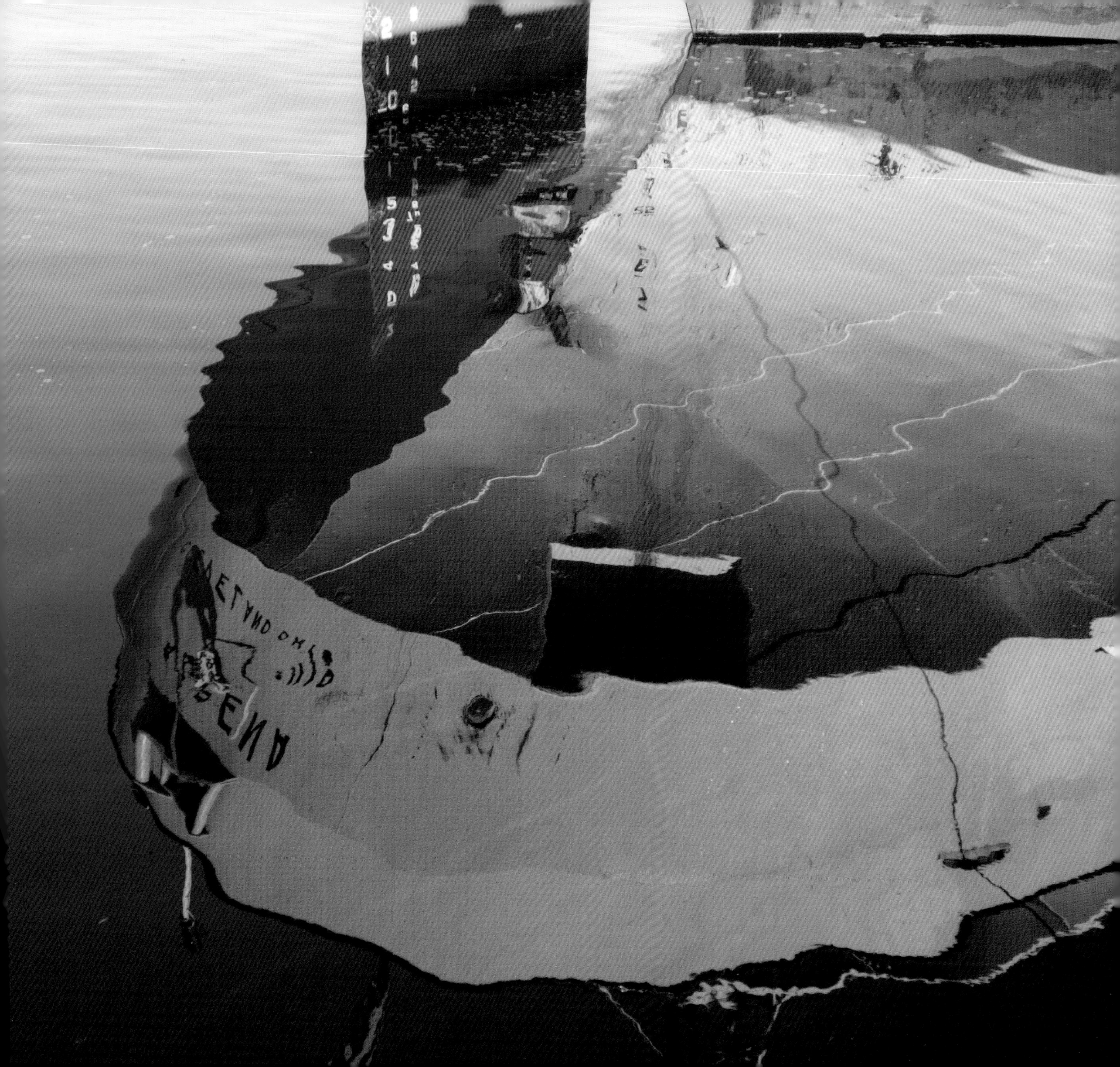

Algocape unloading coal at Dofasco, Hamilton, Ontario, October 2000.

Algorail in full stride, downbound in St. Clair River, Marine City, Michigan, July 2006.

Detail, Lentz Standard Marine Engine,
Cuyahoga, December 1999.

Lentz Standard Marine Engine, *Cuyahoga*, December 1999.

Detail, *Ridgetown*, decommissioned and sunk as break wall, Port Credit, Ontario, June 2004.

Ridgetown, Port Credit, Ontario, June 2004.

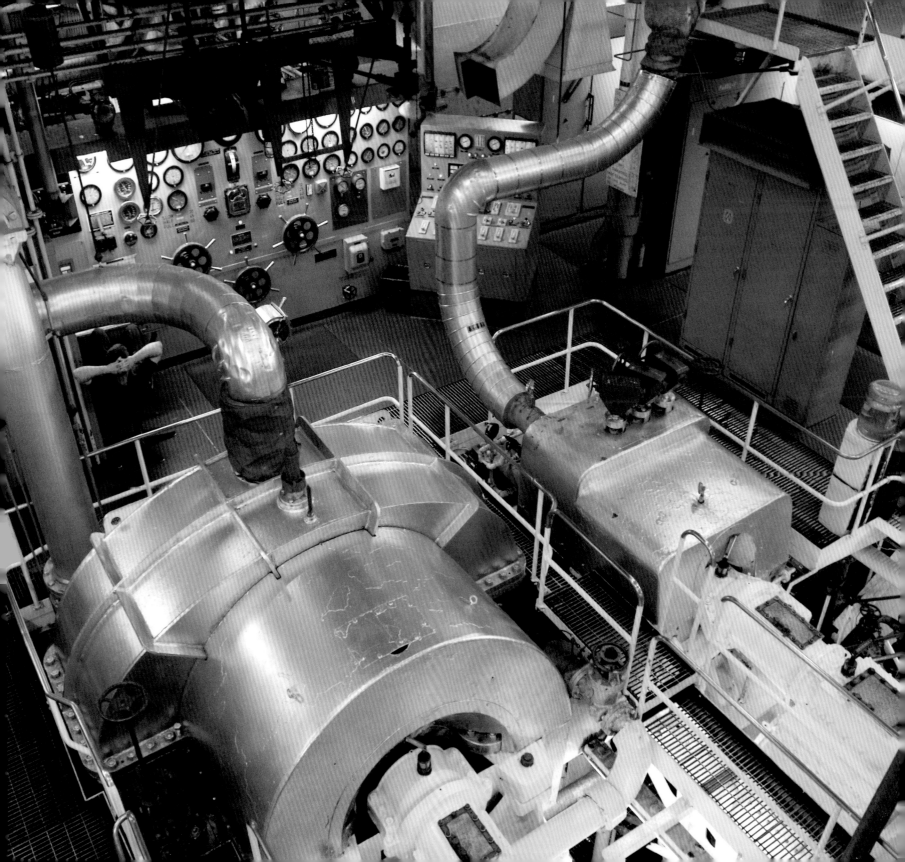

Andy McDonald, fourth engineer, *Saginaw*, September 2005.

Left: DeLaval steam turbine, engine room, *Saginaw*,
Lake Superior, September 2005.

Middletown, downbound, entering St. Clair River at Sarnia, Ontario, August 1999.

BRAD JOLLIFFE

Herbert C. Jackson arriving Marquette, Michigan, August 24, 2002.

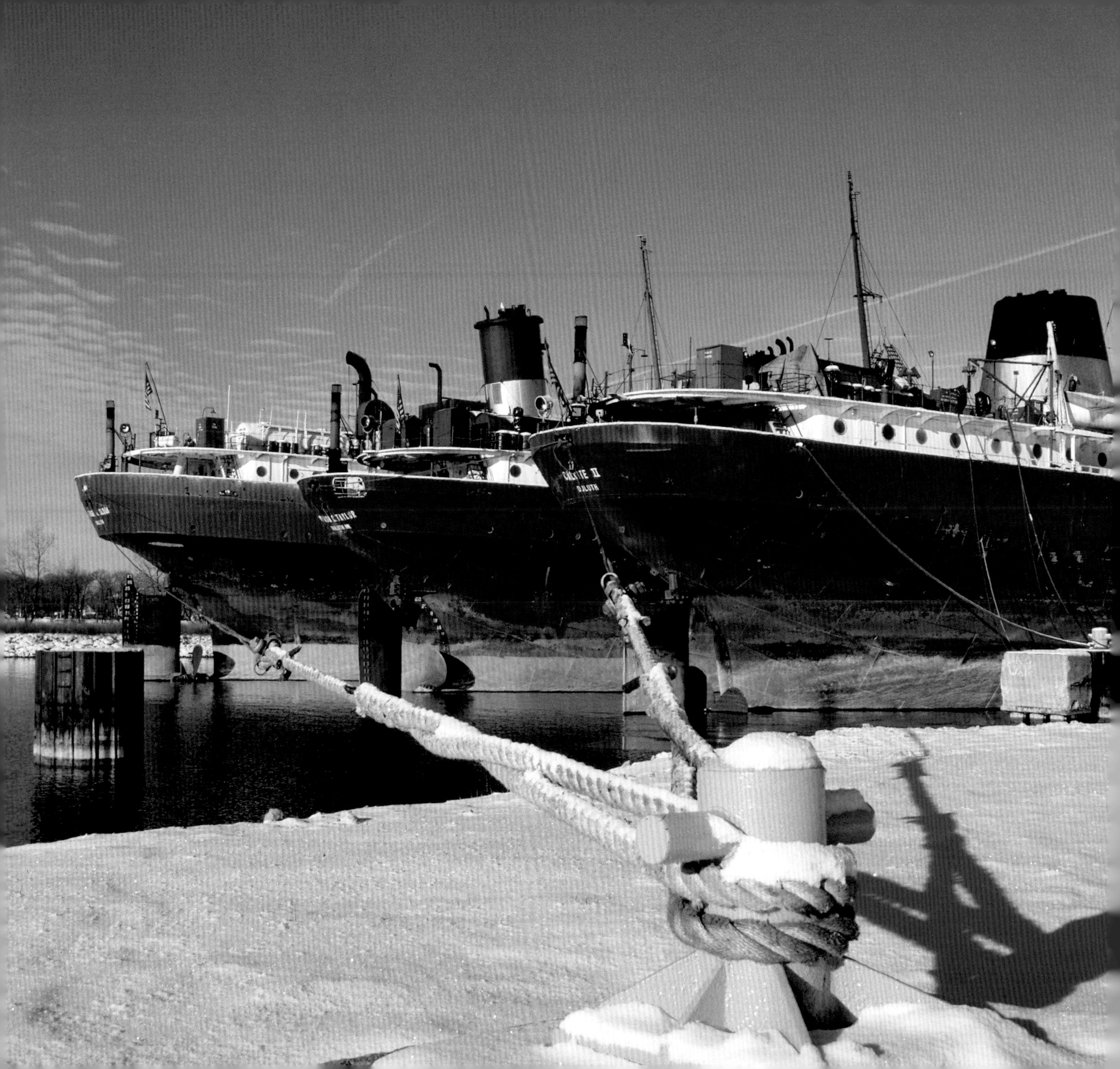

John Sherwin in long-term lay-up, Superior, Wisconsin, August 2006.

Left: *Calcite II, Myron C. Taylor* and *George A. Sloan*
laid-up awaiting refit and revival as
Lower Lakes *Maumee, Calumet*
and *Mississagi*.   BRAD JOLLIFFE

Builder's plate detail, Skinner Marine Unaflow Steam Engine, *St. Marys Challenger,* November 2006.

Detail, Skinner Marine Unaflow Steam Engine, *St. Marys Challenger*, November 2006.

Dennis Hewton, oiler,
Saginaw,
September 2005.

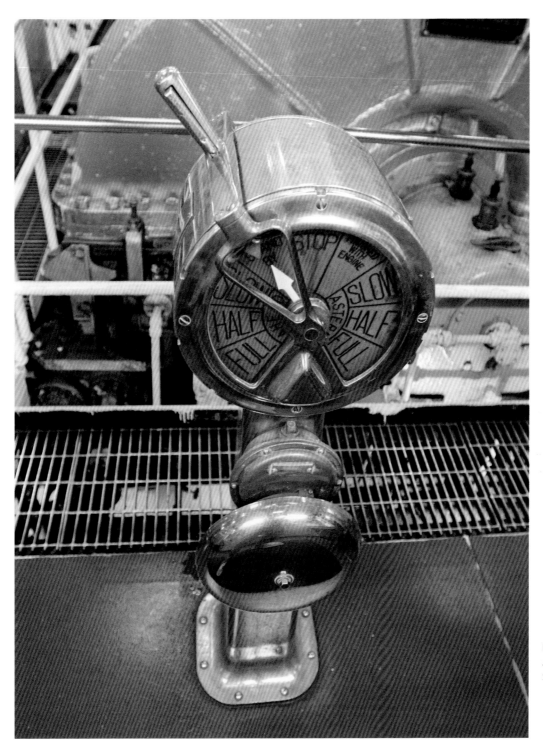

Engine room telegraph,
Saginaw, Lake Superior,
September 2005.

Charles M. Beeghly entering Lake Huron at Sarnia, Ontario, December 2000.

BRAD JOLLIFFE

Maritime Trader upbound in St. Clair River at St. Clair, Michigan, September 2006.

Throttle detail, Skinner Marine Unaflow Steam Engine, *St. Marys Challenger*, November 2006.

Kevin Rogers, third assistant engineer, *St. Marys Challenger*, November 2006.

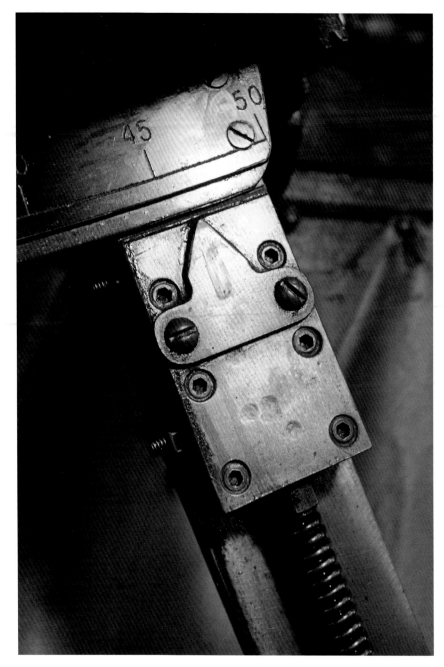

Throttle detail, Skinner Marine Unaflow Steam Engine, *James Norris*, October 2006.

Detail, Vickers-Skinner Marine Unaflow Steam Engine, *James Norris*, October 2006.

Mess, St. Marys Challenger,
November 2006.

Sunset on Lake Michigan, *St. Marys Challenger,* 27 miles out from Milwaukee, Wisconsin, November 2006.

Saginaw, Lake Huron, September 2005.

Saginaw unloading grain, Goderich Elevators, Goderich, Ontario, September 2005.

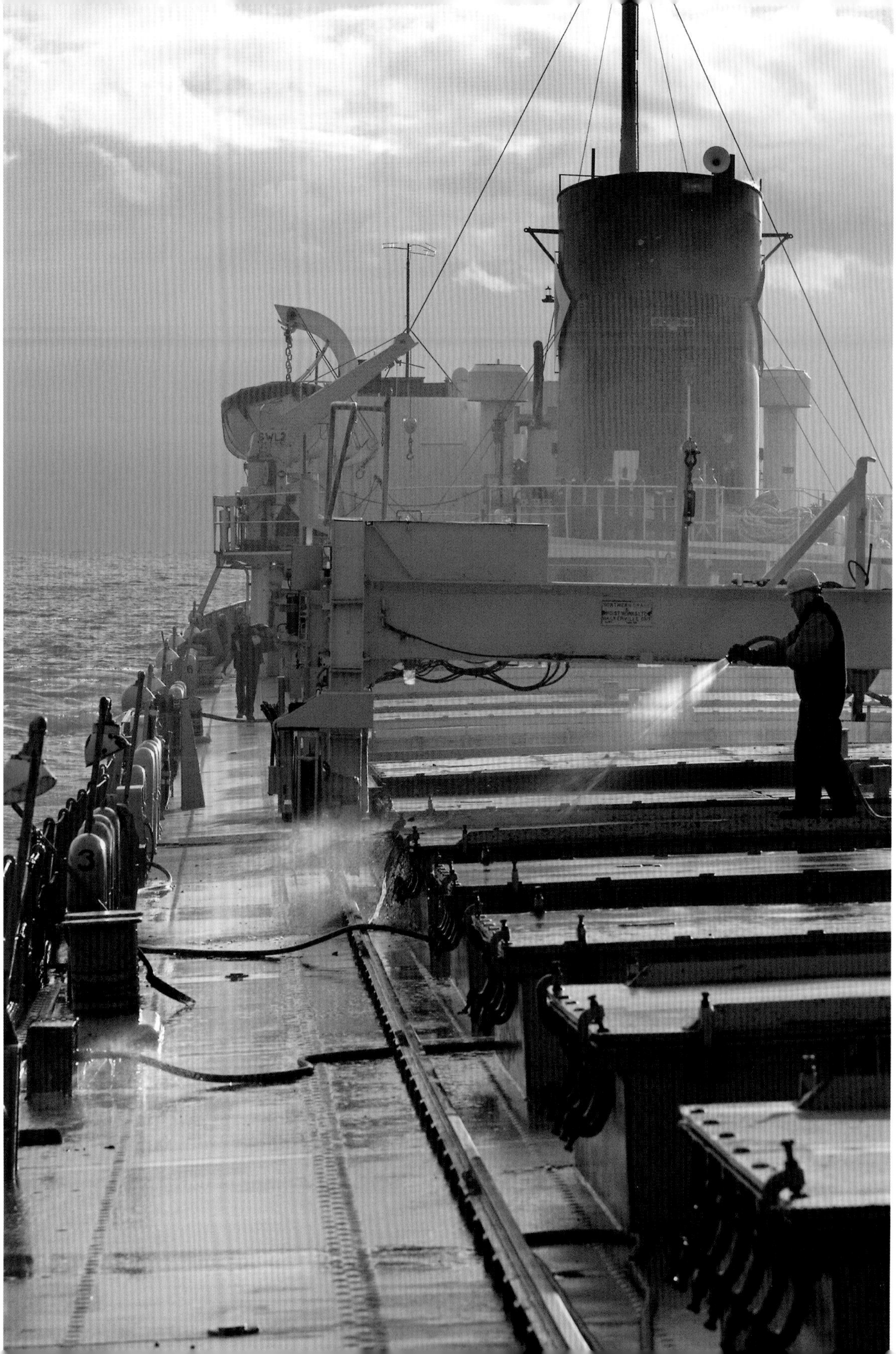

James Norris, October 2006.

Deck detail, *James Norris*, October 2006.

Ed Dewling, captain, *James Norris*, arriving Colborne, Ontario, October 2006.

Detail, pilothouse, *James Norris*, October 2006.

Detail, lubricator, Vickers-Skinner
Marine Unaflow Steam Engine,
James Norris, October 2006.

Tunnel, *James Norris*, October 2006.

Edward L. Ryerson on Detroit River approaching Rouge River, Michigan, October 2006.

M. ROSS VALENTINE

James Norris downbound on Detroit River passing Detroit, Michigan, October 2005.

Detail, engine room, *St. Marys Challenger*, November 2006.

Right: Detail, Skinner Marine Unaflow Steam Engine,
St. Marys Challenger, November 2006.

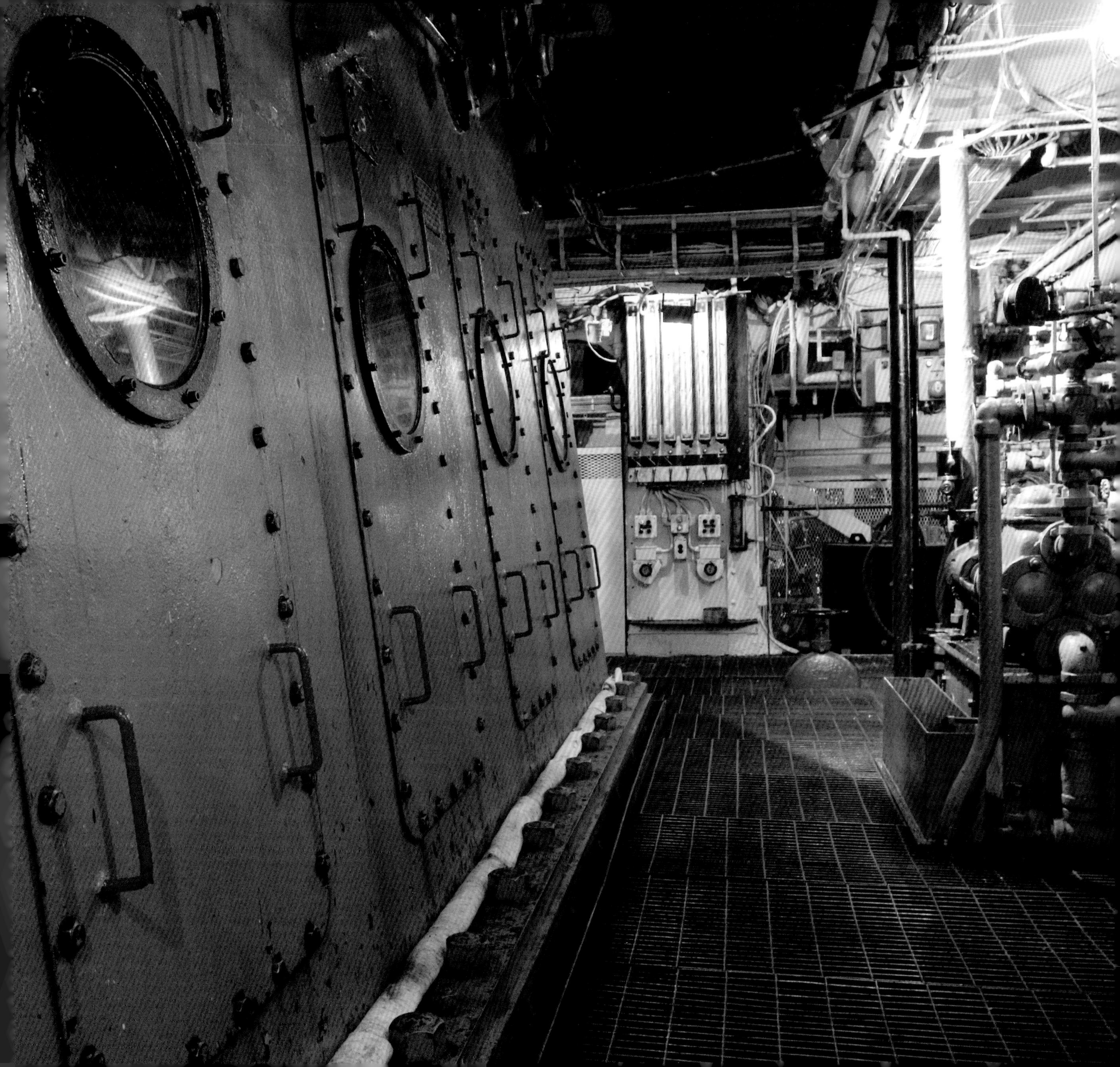

Sam Buchanan pilots mail boat *J.W. Westcott II*, approaching Oglebay Norton for Detroit River mail delivery, Detroit, Michigan, November 2005.

M. ROSS VALENTINE

J.W. Westcott II returning from Detroit River mail delivery to *Manistee*, Detroit, Michigan, June 2005.

Mail by the pail,
J.W. Westcott II
delivering U.S. mail to
Sam Laud on Detroit River,
Detroit, Michigan,
November 2005.
M. ROSS VALENTINE

132

Detail, U.S. mail for *Calumet* aboard *J.W. Westcott II*, November 2005.

S.S. Badger and long-dormant sister *Spartan* at Ludington, Michigan, June 2006.

S.S. Badger arriving Ludington, Michigan.

Deck detail, *Badger*, Ludington, Michigan, October 2004.

Spartan in long-term lay-up,
Ludington, Michigan,
October 2004.

Calumet upbound at
Blue Water Bridge,
Sarnia, Ontario,
August 2002.
MIKE HARTING

138

American Valor downbound on St. Clair River at Walpole Island, Ontario, September 2006.

MIKE HARTING

Mapleglen upbound at Bridge 5, Welland Canal, St. Catharines, Ontario, November 2001.

Canadian Miner downbound in Welland Canal, Bridge 21, Port Colborne, Ontario, August 2001.

Canadian Locomotive Co., Fairbanks Morse opposed-piston engines, *Canadian Miner*, March 2005.

Detail, Fairbanks Morse plate, *Canadian Miner*, March 2005.

Richard Reiss upbound on Detroit River at Detroit, Michigan, September 2004.

JEFF MAST

Richard Reiss on Detroit River at Detroit, Michigan, September 2004.

Charles M. Beeghly downbound on approach to Soo Locks, Sault St. Marie, Michigan, September 2005.

Boat drill on *St. Marys Challenger*, Lake Michigan, November 2006.

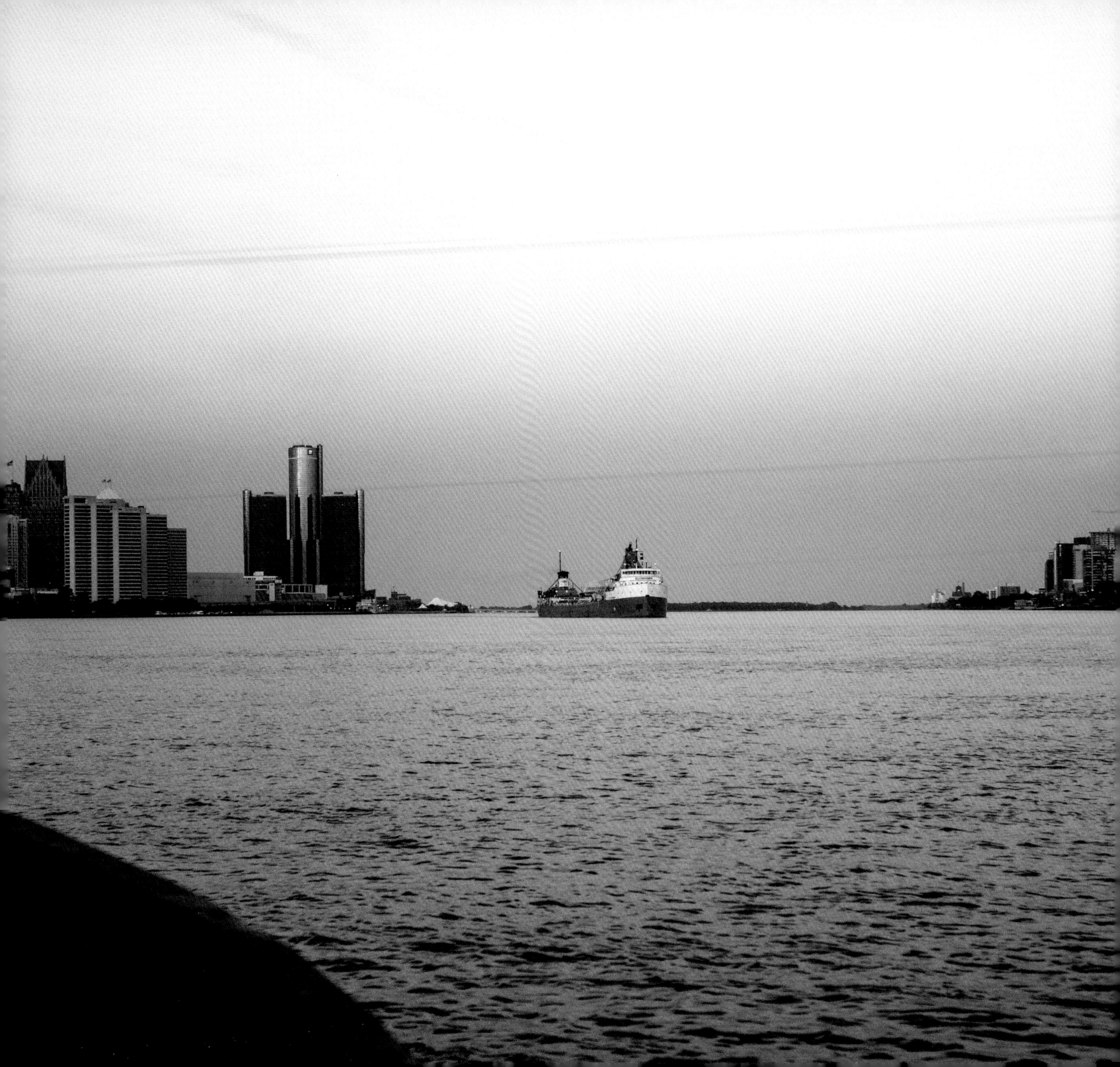

LONG MAY THEY RUN

The Detroit skyline glistens in the crimson glow of a late-summer sundown. Skyscrapers catch the last rays of the setting sun and cast their glint across the fast-moving waters of the Detroit River. It's September 17, 2007, and I'm sitting at a riverfront picnic table at the J.W. Westcott Company dock with a few friends and a box of books: advance copies of the first printing of *Lake Boats*. Hot off the press and delivered by air express for the occasion, they're special copies ordered for contributing photographers, friends and the mariners and shipping companies that helped make the book possible. There seemed no better place from which to ship the books — each one with the title page specially postmarked "Detroit River Sta., MI, 48222" — than from the home of mail boat *J.W. Westcott II*, the only floating United States Post Office and the only boat with its own zip code.

The *J.W. Westcott II* has been engaged in the business of delivering mail, food and supplies, parts, machinery and even crews, ship pilots, and captains to passing vessels since being constructed for the purpose by Paasch Marine Service of Erie, Pennsylvania, in 1949. Westcott Company crews have been providing this unusual but essential service since founder John Ward Westcott ini-

J.W. Westcott II captain Dick Boyle sets his sights on *Cuyahoga*, choreographing a perfect mid-river "mail by the pail" exchange, Detroit, Michigan, September 17, 2007.

tiated mid river "mail by the pail" deliveries with a rowboat in 1874.

The sun is kissing the horizon, and the moon rising over the river as Captain Dick Boyle and the *Westcott II* crew set out with a delivery for the *Cuyahoga*, downbound for Lake Erie. It's a routine run for Boyle and the crew, but I've got a personal stake in the mid-river transaction. The pride of the Lower Lakes Company fleet, *Cuyahoga* (dieselized since our earliest encounters) is an old friend, and an inspiration for the newly printed book tucked in the mail bag about to be hoisted aboard from

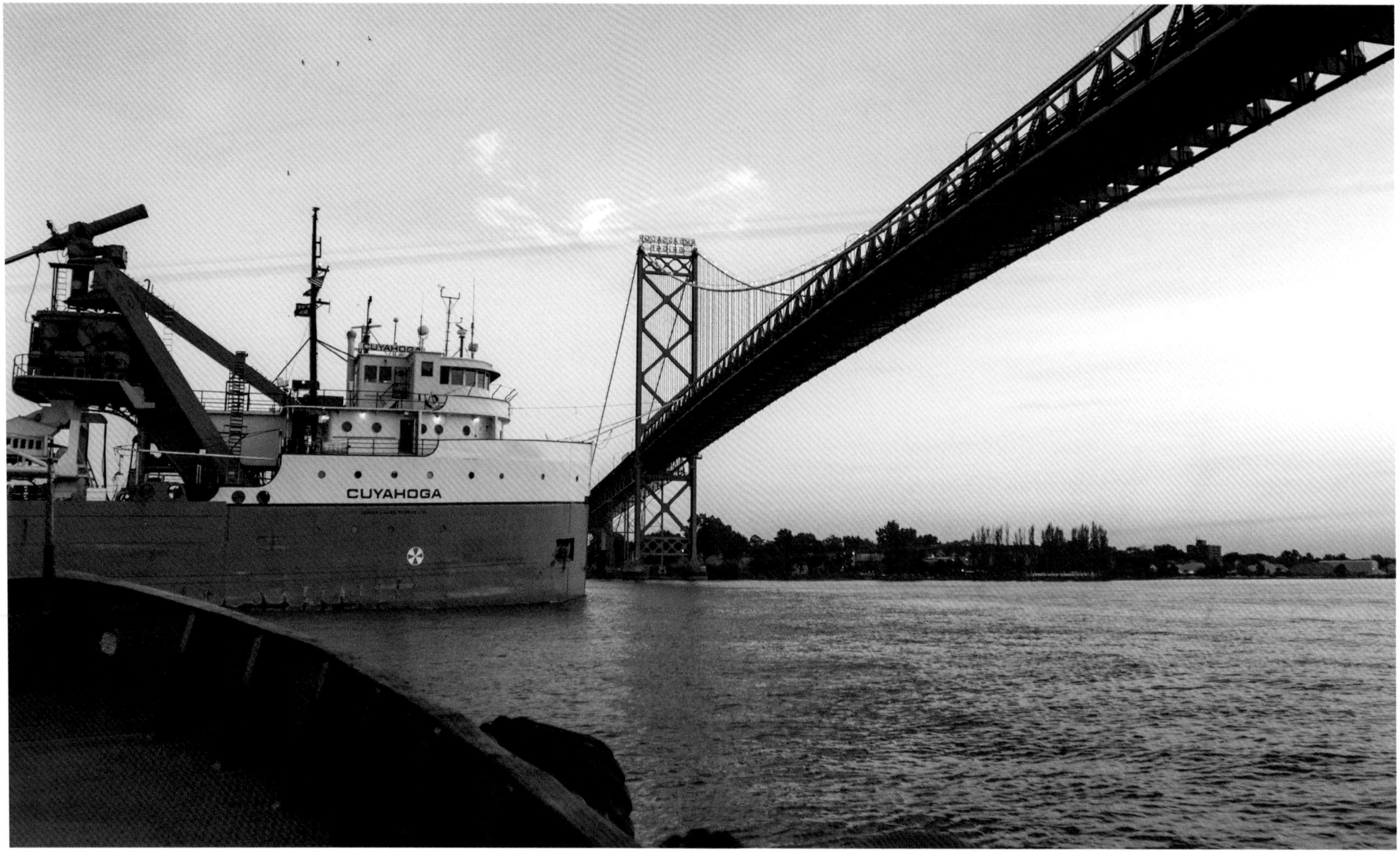
CUYAHOGA

Mail boat *J.W. Westcott II* and *Cuyahoga* approach the Ambassador Bridge, Detroit River, Detroit, Michigan, September 17, 2007.

the *Westcott II*. The connection doesn't stop there. The advance copy of *Lake Boats* is addressed to *Cuyahoga* captain Hugh Pink, who was at the helm of the *Saginaw* for a seven-day Windsor-Sault Ste. Marie-Thunder Bay-Goderich sailing that Brad Jolliffe and I made in the process of making photographs for the book.

Boyle pilots the mail boat in a graceful, perfectly choreographed arc that brings us right alongside *Cuyahoga*. As the two vessels sail side-by-side beneath the Ambassador Bridge, the ritual "mail by the pail" exchange is made. The tiny mail boat keeps pace with the 620-foot-long laker as a *Cuyahoga* crewman lowers a battered pail painted in Lower Lakes' gray, red, white and black stack colors to the deck of the *Westcott II*. The pail is quickly emptied of outgoing mail, stuffed with a bag of incoming mail and returned. A quick wave, and the *Westcott* breaks away. Whistles salute and the *J.W. Westcott II*, zip code 48222, returns to the Detroit River Station.

Nearly seven years have passed since that advance copy of *Lake Boats* was hoisted aboard *Cuyahoga*. Happily, the *J.W. Westcott II* carries on the great tradition of mid-river deliveries and *Cuyahoga* still plies the Lakes under the Lower Lakes flag. Other vessels have been less fortunate.

Time is catching up with the traditional lake boat. In the years since the first edition of this book went to press, more than a dozen have been

Mail by the pail: *Cuyahoga* crewman lowers outbound mail to mail boat *J.W. Westcott II* at sunset, Detroit River, Detroit, Michigan, September 17, 2007.

towed to ship breakers: *Agawa Canyon, Algocape, Canadian Provider, Halifax,* and *Gordon C. Leitch* to name a few, have been towed to Aliaga, Turkey, to be beached and broken up; *Calumet, Canadian Leader, Maumee, James Norris,* and *Quebecois* to the Port Colborne, Ontario, scrap yard operated by International Marine Salvage. The former *Algocen,* which had a miraculous rebirth as *J.W. Shelley,* fell victim to the combined effects of hull damage and bankruptcy and was scrapped mid-repair at Ironhead Shipyard in Toledo, Ohio, after a brief season sailing as the *Phoenix Star.* In what might be considered an attempt to go out in honor, *Canadian Miner,* being towed to the breakers in Aliaga, broke her tow lines in heavy seas, foundered and broke up on the rocky coast of Scatarie Island off Cape Breton, Nova Scotia, in September 2011.

With the demise of the *James Norris* and *Quebecois,* conversion of the 107-year-old *St. Mary's Challenger* to a barge, and the dieselization of vessels including *Kaye E. Barker, Charles M. Beeghly, Michipicoten* and *Saginaw,* steam-powered lake boats have become endangered species. Only seven steam-driven freighters remain on the lakes, and at last report, most are laid up.

Keep the faith. Canadian and U.S. concerns still flag a handful of pure straight-deckers, many more live on converted to self-unloaders. While conversion of conventional lake boats to self-unloaders might mar their classic lines, the life-extending efficiencies are undeniable. And each year, from mid-May to the end of October, steam courses through the 4-cylinder Skinner Marine Unaflow engines of the coal-fired S.S. *Badger* as the last reciprocating-steam powered vessel on the Great Lakes ferries passengers and vehicles across Lake Michigan from Ludington, Michigan, to Manitowoc, Wisconsin.

Scott Bravener's adopted Lower Lakes motto is more appropriate than ever. Don't give up the ship.

Cuyahoga and moonrise over the Detroit River, Detroit, Michigan, at sunset, September 17, 2007.

CSL Tadoussac, Sarnia, Ontario, August 8, 2011.

J.W. Shelley, upbound on maiden trip, meets downbound *Algomarine*, at Lock 6 on the Welland Canal, Thorold, Ontario, September 8, 2008.

American Valor, downbound, Detroit, Michigan, September 18, 2007.

Canadian Provider approaching the Ambassador Bridge at Windsor/Detroit, June 3, 2010.

JEFF MAST

Alpena, Lake Huron Cut, Port Huron, Michigan, March 20, 2010.

JEFF MAST

Saginaw, St. Clair River, Marysville, Michigan, March 21, 2010.

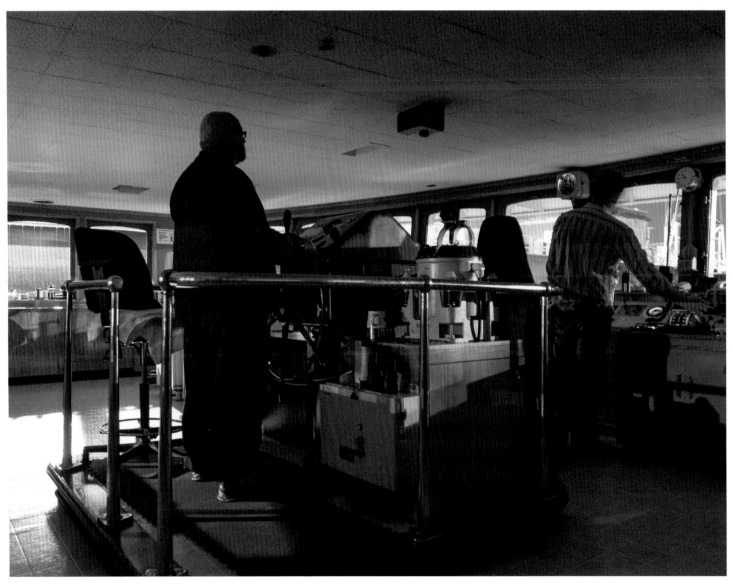

Captain Ed Dewling at the helm of *Canadian Miner*, transiting the Welland Canal, Quebec-bound on Trip 7024 with 26,024.97 metric tonnes of wheat from Thunder Bay, November 25, 2007.

Canadian Miner, at Lock 4 of
the Welland Canal, Thorold,
Ontario, November 25, 2007.

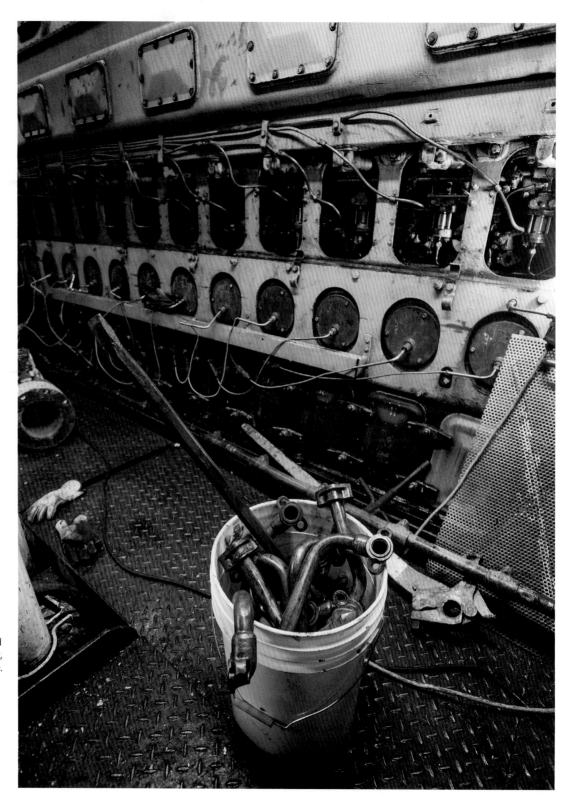

Fairbanks-Morse engines being stripped for parts, *Canadian Miner*, Cherry Street, Toronto, Ontario, July 29, 2010.

Canadian Miner awaiting disposition at Cherry Street, Toronto, Ontario, July 29, 2010.

Algoma Mariner, upbound in ballast, Lock 7 Welland Canal, Thorold, Ontario, December 15, 2010.

Detail with ice, *Algoma Mariner*, Welland Canal, Thorold, Ontario, December 15, 2010.

St. Mary's Challenger, Owen Sound, Ontario, September 12, 2013.

BRAD JOLLIFFE

Ojibway, Owen Sound, Ontario, September 19, 2013.

BRAD JOLLIFFE

Phoenix Star, downbound at Welland Canal Bridge 5, St. Catharines, Ontario, September 07, 2012.

Algoma Provider, transiting Welland Canal, downbound at Bridge 5, St. Catharines, Ontario, November 27, 2012.

Gordon C. Leitch departing Hamilton, Ontario, October 18, 2011.

Milwaukee morning. *Manistee* arriving at Milwaukee, Wisconsin at dawn, November 12, 2010.

Montrealais at Dofasco ore dock, Hamilton, Ontario, November 11, 2007.

Montrealais unloading 26,000 tons of Pointe Noire iron ore at Dofasco, Hamilton, Ontario, November 11, 2007.

Ore boats. *Michipicoten* and *Kaye E. Barker* at LS&I ore dock, Marquette, Michigan, October 23, 2010.

JEFF MAST

Chief engineer George Lundrigan and engine room Chadburn, *S.S. Michipicoten*, in winter lay up Pier 11W, Hamilton, Ontario, January 6, 2009.

Edward L. Ryerson, upbound at Welland Canal Lock 7, Thorold, Ontario, October 22, 2008.

Edward L. Ryerson, in long-term layup,
Fraser's Ship Yard, Superior, Wisconsin,
August 14, 2013.

Michipicoten arriving at Algoma Steel, Sault Ste. Marie, Ontario, October 24, 2010.

St. Mary's Challenger arriving Charlevoix, Michigan, July 28, 2012.

JEFF MAST

Algomarine and *Peter R. Creswell* in winter lay-up. Goderich, Ontario, February 2007.

MASTER'S LIST

AGAWA CANYON
- Algoma Central Corporation, Sault Ste. Marie, Ontario
- Self-unloader

Built: Collingwood Shipyards, Collingwood, Ontario, 1970
Length: 646' 8"
Beam: 72' 3"
Depth: 40'
Capacity at mid-summer draft: 24,050 tons
Propulsion: diesel
Engines/horsepower — original: 8064 b.h.p. from four 10-cylinder, 1666 b.h.p. Fairbanks-Morse 38D 8 1/8 opposed-piston engines and two 700 b.h.p., 12-cylinder Caterpillar engines
Engines/horsepower — current: 6664 b.h.p. from four 10-cylinder, 1666-b.h.p Fairbanks-Morse 38D 8 1/8 opposed-piston engines built by Canadian Locomotive Co., Kingston, Ontario
Lineage:
- 1970–2010: *Agawa Canyon*, Algoma Central Corporation, Sault Ste. Marie, Ontario

Notes: Launched at Collingwood Shipyards, Collingwood, Ontario, August 27, 1970. Re-powered in 1975 with four 10-cylinder, Fairbanks-Morse 38D 8 1/8 opposed-piston engines built by Canadian Locomotive Co., Kingston, Ontario. Winter layup in Montreal, Que., December 22, 2009. Towed to Aliaga, Turkey for scrap, September 2010.

ALGOCAPE
- Algoma Central Corporation, Sault Ste. Marie, Ontario
- Straight-deck bulk carrier

Built: Davie Shipbuilding Ltd., Lauzon, Quebec, 1967
Length: 729' 9"
Beam: 75' 4"
Depth: 39' 8"
Capacity at mid-summer draft: 29,950 tons
Propulsion: diesel
Engine/Horsepower: 8500 b.h.p., 6-cylinder Sulzer 6RND76
Lineage:
- 1967–1994: *Richelieu*, Canada Steamship Lines, Montreal, Quebec
- 1994–2012: *Algocape* (second), Algoma Central Corporation,

Sault Ste. Marie, Ontario.
Notes: Launched at Davie Shipbuilding, Lauzon, Quebec, November 25, 1966 as Canada Steamship Lines *Richelieu*. Acquired by Algoma Central Corporation in 1994 and renamed *Algocape*. Winter layup in Montreal, Que., December 22, 2011. Towed to Aliaga, Turkey for scrap, August 2012.

ALGOMA PROVIDER — see Canadian Provider

ALGOMARINE
- Algoma Central Corporation, Sault Ste. Marie, Ontario
- Straight-deck bulk carrier; conversion from straight-deck bulk carrier

Built: Davie Shipbuilding Ltd., Lauzon, Quebec, 1968
Length: 730'
Beam: 75'
Depth: 39' 8"
Capacity at mid-summer draft: 27,000 tons
Propulsion: diesel
Engine/Horsepower: 9470 b.h.p., 6-cylinder Sulzer 6RND76
Lineage:
- 1968–1986: Lake Manitoba, Nipigon Transports Ltd., Montreal, Quebec; managed by Carryore Ltd.
- 1986–1987: Lake Manitoba, Algoma Central Corporation, Sault Ste. Marie, Ontario
- 1987–present: Algomarine, Algoma Central Corporation, Sault Ste. Marie, Ontario

Notes: Built by Davie Shipbuilding, Lauzon, Quebec, in 1968 as Nipigon Transports Lake Manitoba. Acquired by Algoma Central Corporation in 1986; renamed Algomarine in 1987. Converted to self-unloader at Port Weller Dry Docks in 1988.

ALGORAIL
- Algoma Central Corporation, Sault Ste. Marie, Ontario
- Self-unloader Built: Collingwood Shipyards, Collingwood, Ontario, 1968

Length: 640' 5"
Beam: 72' 3"
Depth: 40'
Capacity at mid-summer draft: 23, 750 tons
Propulsion: diesel

Engine/Horsepower: 6664 b.h.p. from four 10-cylinder, 1666-b.h.p Fairbanks-Morse 38D 8 1/8 opposed-piston engines built by Canadian Locomotive Co., Kingston, Ontario
Lineage:
- 1968–present: *Algorail* (second), Algoma Central Corporation, Sault Ste. Marie, Ontario

Notes: Built by Collingwood Shipyards, Collingwood, Ontario, and christened *Algorail* at Collingwood on April 1, 1968.

ALGOSTEEL
- Algoma Central Corporation, Sault Ste. Marie, Ontario
- Self-unloader; conversion from straight-deck bulk carrier

Built: Davie Shipbuilding, Inc., Lauzon, Quebec, 1966
Length: 729' 11"
Beam: 75'
Depth: 39' 8"
Capacity at mid-summer draft: 26,534 tons
Propulsion: diesel
Engine/Horsepower: 9470 b.h.p., 6-cylinder Sulzer 6RND76
Lineage:
- 1966–1971: *A.S. Glossbrenner*, Labrador Steamship Co., Montreal, Quebec
- 1971–1987: *A.S. Glossbrenner*, Algoma Central Corporation, Sault Ste. Marie, Ontario
- 1987–1990: *Algogulf* (1st), Algoma Central Corporation, Sault Ste. Marie, Ontario
- 1990–present: *Algosteel*, Algoma Central Corporation, Sault Ste. Marie, Ontario

Notes: Built as *A.S. Glossbrenner* for Labrador Steamship Co., Montreal, Quebec. Sold to Algoma Central Corp., 1971, retaining original name. Converted to self-unloader in 1990 and renamed *Algosteel*. Second Algoma Central vessel to carry this name.

ALPENA
- Inland Lakes Management, Alpena, Michigan
- Cement carrier

Built: Great Lakes Engineering Works, River Rouge, Michigan, 1942
Length: 519' 6" (shortened from 639' 6")
Beam: 67'

Hull detail, Algoma Central Marine, *Algosteel*, October 2005.

Depth: 35'
Capacity at mid-summer draft: 13,900 tons
Propulsion: steam turbine
Engine/Horsepower: 4400 s.h.p., DeLaval cross-compound steam turbine built by DeLaval Steam Turbine Co., Trenton, New Jersey.
Lineage:
* 1942–1985: *Leon Fraser*, Pittsburgh Steamship Co., Cleveland, Ohio
* 1985–1989: *Leon Fraser*, Spitzer Marine (not in service)
* 1989–1990: *Leon Fraser*, Fraser Shipyards, Inc., Superior, Wisconsin
* 1991–present: *Alpena*, Inland Lakes Transportation, Alpena, Michigan

Notes: Launched February 28, 1942 as Pittsburgh Steamship Co., *Leon Fraser* at Great Lakes Engineering Works, Rouge River, Michigan. Sailed in U.S. Steel fleet until laid up in 1982 at former American Ship Building Co., yard in Lorain, Ohio. Sold to Spitzer Marine, Inc., in 1989, and then to Fraser Shipyards, Inc., in October 1989. Moved to Fraser's Superior, Wisconsin, facility for rebuild to self-unloading cement carrier. Shortened by 120 feet during rebuild; sold to Inland Lakes Transportation in 1990. Christened *Alpena* June 10, 1991 and returned to service in cement trade.

AMERICAN VALOR
* American Steamship Co., Williamsville, New York
* Self-unloader, conversion from straight-deck bulk carrier
Built: American Ship Building Co., Lorain, Ohio, 1953
Length: 767'
Beam: 70'
Depth: 36'
Capacity at mid-summer draft: 25,500 tons

Propulsion: steam turbine
Engine/Horsepower: 7700 s.h.p. cross-compound steam turbine built by Westinghouse Electric Corporation, Philadelphia, Pennsylvania
Lineage:
* 1953–1994: *Armco*, Columbia Transportation Division, Oglebay Norton Co., Cleveland, Ohio
* 1994–2006: *Armco*, Oglebay Norton Co., Cleveland, Ohio
* 2006–present: *American Valor*, American Steamship Co., Williamsville, New York

Notes: Constructed by American Ship Building Co., Lorain, Ohio, as Columbia Transportation Division, Oglebay Norton Co., *Armco*. Lengthened by 120 feet at Fraser Shipyards, Superior, Wisconsin in 1974. Converted to self-unloader at Bay Shipyards, Sturgeon Bay, Wisconsin in 1982. Sold, along with five fleet mates, to American Steamship Co., Williamsville, New York, in June 2006 and renamed *American Valor*. Laid up, Toledo, Ohio, November 11, 2008.

AMERICAN VICTORY
* American Steamship Co., Williamsville, New York
* Self-unloader, conversion from straight-deck bulk carrier
Built: Bethlehem Steel Corporation, Sparrows Point, Maryland, 1942
Length: 730
Beam: 75'
Depth: 39' 3"
Capacity at mid-summer draft: 26,300 tons
Propulsion: steam turbine
Engine/Horsepower: 7700 s.h.p. steam turbine built by Bethlehem Steel Co., Quincy, Massachusetts
Lineage:
* 1942–1943: USS *Marquette*, United States Navy (constructed as tanker)
* 1943–1947: USS *Neshanic*, AO-71, United States Navy
* 1947–1958: *Gulfoil*, Gulf Oil Co.
* 1958–1961: out of service after collision and fire; being rebuilt
* 1961–1962: *Pioneer Challenger*, Pioneer Steamship Co., Cleveland, Ohio
* 1962–1994: *Middletown*, Columbia Transportation Division, Oglebay Norton Co., Cleveland, Ohio
* 1994–2006: *Middletown*, Oglebay Norton Co., Cleveland, Ohio
* 2006–present: *American Victory*, American Steamship Co., Williamsville, New York

Notes: Constructed as "oiler" for U.S. Navy by Bethlehem Steel Corporation at Sparrows Point, Maryland in 1942. Launched as *Marquette*, but commissioned as USS *Neshanic* in April 1943. Served in Atlantic and Pacific theatres during World War II; damaged in Japanese aerial attack on June 18, 1944. Decommissioned December 1945; sold to Gulf Oil co., and renamed *Gulfoil* in 1947. Severely damaged by fire and most of crew killed, in collision with tanker *S.E. Graham* near

Newport, Rhode Island, August 7, 1958. Rebuilt — with new mid-section constructed by Verolme United Shipyards, Rotterdam, Holland — as straight-deck bulk carrier by Maryland Shipbuilding & Drydock Co., Baltimore, Maryland, 1959–60. Entered Great Lakes service as Pioneer Steamship Co., *Pioneer Challenger*, in July 1961. Purchased by Columbia Transportation Division, Oglebay Norton Co., following dissolution of Pioneer fleet in 1961, and renamed *Middletown*. Converted to self-unloader by Bay Shipbuilding, Sturgeon Bay, Wisconsin, in 1982. Sold, along with five fleet mates, to American Steamship Co., Williamsville, New York, June 6, 2006 and renamed *American Victory*. Laid up Superior, Wisconsin, November 12, 2008.

ARMCO — see American Valor

ARTHUR M. ANDERSON
* Great Lakes Fleet, Inc., Duluth, Minnesota
* Self-unloader,
Built: American Ship Building Co., Lorain, Ohio, 1952
Length: 767' (lengthened from 647')
Beam: 70'
Depth: 36'
Capacity at mid-summer draft: 25,300 tons
Propulsion: steam turbine
Engine/Horsepower: 7700 s.h.p. steam turbine built by Westinghouse Electric Corporation, Philadelphia, Pennsylvania
Lineage:
* 1952–2004: United States Steel Corp., Great Lakes Fleet
* 2004–present: *Arthur M. Anderson*, CN-Great Lakes Fleet Inc., Duluth, Minnesota; operated by Keystone Shipping Co., Bala Cynwyd, Pennsylvania

Notes: Launched February 16, 1952 at American Ship Building Co., Lorain, Ohio, as U.S. Steel Great Lakes Fleet *Arthur M. Anderson*. Lengthened by 120 feet by Fraser Shipyards, Superior, Wisconsin, during winter lay-up 1974–75. Converted to self-unloader at Fraser Shipyards during winter lay-up 1981–82. Noted for role in search and rescue attempts during storm that claimed *Edmund Fitzgerald*, November 10, 1975.

S.S. BADGER
* Lake Michigan Carferry Service Inc., Ludington, Michigan
* Car ferry
Built: Christy Corporation, Sturgeon Bay, Wisconsin, 1952
Length: 410' 6"
Beam: 59' 6"
Depth: 24'
Capacity: 620 passengers, 180 automobiles
Propulsion: steam
Engine/Horsepower: 7000 b.h.p. from two 3500-i.h.p., steeple-compound, 4-cylinder Skinner Marine Unaflow engines built by Skinner Engine Co., Erie, Pennsylvania

Stack detail, *Alpena*, Match 2006.

Lineage:
- 1953–1983: S.S. *Badger*, Chesapeake & Ohio Railway
- 1983–1991: S.S. *Badger*, Wisconsin-Michigan Transportation Co.
- 1991–present: S.S. *Badger*, Lake Michigan Carferry Service Inc., Ludington, Michigan

Notes: S.S. *Badger* built for Chesapeake & Ohio Railway Lake Michigan car ferry service by Christy Corporation, Sturgeon Bay, Wisconsin. Launched in September 1952. Operated car ferry service transporting rail cars, motor vehicles and passengers between Ludington, Michigan, and Milwaukee, Manitowoc and Kewaunee, Wisconsin. Sold to Wisconsin-Michigan Transportation Co., in 1983. Rail shipments ended in 1988; service discontinued in 1990. Purchased by Lake Michigan Carferry Service, reconditioned and returned to service, May 15, 1992. Engines and boilers declared historical mechanical engineering landmark by American Society of Mechanical Engineers, September 1996. Last coal-fired vessel operating on the Great Lakes.

KAYE E. BARKER
- Lakes Shipping Co., Division of Interlake Steamship Co., Richfield, Ohio
- Self-unloader, conversion from straight-deck bulk carrier

Built: American Ship Building Co., Toledo, Ohio, 1952
Length: 767'
Beam: 70'
Depth: 36'
Capacity at mid-summer draft: 25,900 tons
Propulsion: diesel
Engine/Horsepower — original: 7700 s.h.p., DeLaval cross-compound steam turbine built by DeLaval Steam Turbine Co., Trenton, New Jersey.
Engines/horsepower — current: 8160 b.h.p from two Rolls-Royce Bergen B32:40L6P 6-cylinder engines.
Lineage:
- 1952–1985: *Edward B. Greene*, Cleveland Cliffs Steamship Co.
- 1985–1989: *Benson Ford*, Rouge Steel Co.
- 1990–present: *Kaye E. Barker*, Lakes Shipping Co., division of Interlake Steamship Co., Richfield, Ohio

Notes: Built by American Ship Building Co., Toledo, Ohio, in 1952 as Cleveland Cliffs Steamship Co., *Edward B. Greene*. Lengthened by 120 feet from as-built 647 feet to 767 feet at Fraser Shipyards, Superior, Wisconsin, during winter 1975–76. Converted to self-unloader, American Ship Building Co., Toledo, Ohio, during winter 1980–81. Sold to Ford Motor Co., subsidiary Rouge Steel Co., in 1985 and renamed *Benson Ford*, the third Rouge vessel to carry the name. Ford fleet dissolved in 1989 and taken over by Lakes Shipping Co., division of Interlake Steamship Co., *Benson Ford* renamed *Kaye E. Barker*, August 2, 1990. Conversion from steam to diesel performed by Bay Shipbuilding, Sturgeon Bay, Wisc., in 2012.

CHARLES M. BEEGHLY
- Interlake Steamship Co., Richfield, Ohio
- Self-unloader, conversion from straight-deck bulk carrier

Built: American Ship Building Co., Toledo, Ohio, 1959
Length: 806' (lengthened from 710')
Beam: 75'
Depth: 37' 6"
Capacity at mid-summer draft: 31,000 tons
Propulsion: diesel
Engine/Horsepower: 9350 s.h.p., cross-compound steam turbine built by General Electric Co., Schenectady, New York.
Engines/horsepower — current: 8158 b.h.p from two Rolls-Royce Bergen B32:40L6P 6-cylinder engines.
Lineage:
- 1959–1967: *Shenango II*, Shenango Furnace Co., Pittsburgh, Pennsylvania
- 1967–2011: *Charles M. Beeghly* — Interlake Steamship Co., Richfield, Ohio
- 2011–present: *Hon. James L. Oberstar* — Interlake Steamship Co., Richfield, Ohio

Notes: Built in 1959 by American Ship Building Co., Toledo, Ohio, as Shenango Furnace Co., *Shenango II*. Sold to Interlake Steamship Co., March 1, 1967 and renamed *Charles M. Beeghly*. Additional hold added to vessel at Fraser Shipyards, Superior, Wisconsin, during winter lay-up 1971–72; length increased by 96 feet. Converted to self-unloader during winter of 1980–81 by Fraser Shipyards. Conversion from steam to diesel performed by Bay Shipbuilding, Sturgeon Bay, Wisc., in 2008–2009. Renamed *Hon. James L. Oberstar* at Detroit, Mich., March 7, 2011.

COURTNEY BURTON
- Oglebay Norton Co., Cleveland, Ohio
- Self-unloader; conversion from straight-deck bulk carrier

Built: American Ship Building Co., Lorain, Ohio, 1953
Length: 690'
Beam: 70'
Depth: 37'
Capacity at mid-summer draft: 22,300 tons
Propulsion: steam turbine
Engine/Horsepower: 7700 s.h.p., cross-compound steam turbine built by General Electric Co., Lynn Massachusetts.
Lineage:
- 1953–1978: *Ernest T. Weir* (second), National Steel Corp., Cleveland, Ohio
- 1978: *Ernest T. Weir*, Columbia Transportation Division, Oglebay Norton Co., Cleveland, Ohio
- 1978–1994: *Courtney Burton*, Columbia Transportation Division, Oglebay Norton Co., Cleveland, Ohio
- 1994–2006: *Courtney Burton*, Oglebay Norton Co., Cleveland, Ohio
- 2006–present: *American Fortitude*, American Steamship Co., Williamsville, New York

Notes: Built by American Ship Building Co., Lorain, Ohio, as National Steel Corp., *Ernest T. Weir* in 1953. Boilers converted from coal-burning to oil-fired at Bay Shipbuilding, Sturgeon Bay, Wisconsin, during winter 1972–73. Sold in 1978 to Columbia Transportation Division, Oglebay Norton Co., Cleveland, Ohio. Operated through 1978 as *Ernest T. Weir*; renamed *Courtney Burton* in December 1978. Converted to self-unloader by Bay Shipbuilding, Sturgeon Bay, Wisconsin, during 1980–81. Sold, along with five fleet mates, to American Steamship Co., Williamsville, New York, in June 2006 and renamed *American Fortitude*. Laid up Toledo, Ohio, November 11, 2008.

CASON J. CALLAWAY
- Great Lakes Fleet, Inc., Duluth, Minnesota
- Self-unloader; conversion from straight-deck bulk carrier

Built: Great Lakes Engineering Works, River Rouge, Michigan, 1952
Length: 767' (lengthened from 647')
Beam: 70'

Depth: 36'
Capacity at mid-summer draft: 25,300 tons
Propulsion: steam turbine
Engine/Horsepower: 7700 s.h.p. steam turbine built by Westinghouse Electric Corporation, Philadelphia, Pennsylvania
Lineage:
- 1952–1981: *Cason J. Callaway*, Pittsburgh Steamship Co., Cleveland, Ohio
- 1981–2004: *Cason J. Callaway*, USS Great Lakes Fleet, Cleveland, Ohio
- 2004–present: *Cason J. Callaway*, CN-Great Lakes Fleet Inc., operated by Keystone Shipping Co., Bala Cynwyd, Pennsylvania

Notes: *Cason J. Callaway* constructed in 1952 by Great Lakes Engineering Works, River Rouge, Michigan, for U.S. Steel's Pittsburgh Steamship Co. Lengthened by 120 feet by Fraser Shipyards, Superior, Wisconsin, during winter lay-up 1974–75. Converted to self-unloader at Fraser Shipyards during winter lay-up 1981–82. Canadian National Railway acquired USS Great Lakes Fleet in 2004; fleet operated by Keystone Shipping Co., Bala Cynwyd, Pennsylvania.

CALUMET (SECOND)
- Grand River Navigation/Lower Lakes Transportation Co., Cleveland, Ohio
- Self-unloader; conversion from straight-deck bulk carrier

Built: Great Lakes Engineering Works, River Rouge, Michigan, 1929
Length: 603' 9"
Beam: 60'
Depth: 32'
Capacity at mid-summer draft: 12,450 tons
Propulsion — as built: steam
Propulsion — current: diesel
Engine/Horsepower — original: 2200 i.h.p., triple-expansion, Great Lakes Engineering Works, River Rouge, Michigan
Engine/Horsepower — current: 4336 b.h.p., 16-cylinder Nordberg FS-1316-H5C built by Nordberg Manufacturing Co., Milwaukee, Wisconsin
Lineage:
- 1929–1956: *Myron C. Taylor*, Pittsburgh Steamship Co., Cleveland, Ohio
- 1956–1967: *Myron C. Taylor*, Bradley Transportation Co., Rogers City, Michigan, managed by Pittsburgh Steamship
- 1967–1981: *Myron C. Taylor*, Pittsburgh Steamship Co., Cleveland, Ohio
- 1981–2001: *Myron C. Taylor*, USS Great Lakes Fleet, Cleveland, Ohio
- 2001–2007: *Calumet*, Grand River Navigation/ Lower Lakes Transportation Co., Cleveland, Ohio

Notes: *Myron C. Taylor* constructed by Great Lakes Engineering

Works, River Rouge, Michigan, in 1929 for U.S. Steel's Pittsburgh Steamship Co., Cleveland Ohio. Reassigned to Pittsburgh Steamship-managed Bradley Transportation Co., Rogers City, Michigan, in 1956. Converted to self-unloader by Christy Corp., Sturgeon Bay, Wisconsin, in summer of 1956. Sailed again under Pittsburgh Steamship flag as Bradley and Pittsburgh fleets merged July 1, 1967 by U.S. Steel. Dieselized in 1968 with 16-cylinder engine built by Nordberg Manufacturing Co., Milwaukee, Wisconsin. Re-flagged again when USS Great Lakes Fleet created in June 1981. Laid-up at Sarnia, Ontario, November 11, 2000, in anticipation of sale to U.S. subsidiary of Lower Lakes Towing. Sold with fleet mates *Calcite II* and *George A. Sloan* to Lower Lakes affiliate Grand River Navigation Co., Cleveland, Ohio, March 2001. Christened *Calumet* at Sarnia, April 21, 2001. Vessel due for retirement in 2007. Damage inflicted in contact with concrete wall on Old River in Cleveland, Ohio, on November 15, 2007 advanced removal from service. Repaired and moved to International Marine Salvage, Port Colborne, Ontario, for scrap on November 20, 2007.

CANADIAN LEADER
- Upper Lakes Shipping, Toronto, Ontario
- Straight-deck bulk carrier

Built: Collingwood Shipyards, Collingwood, Ontario, 1967
Length: 730'
Beam: 75'
Depth: 39' 8"
Capacity at mid-summer draft: 28,300 tons
Propulsion: steam turbine
Engine/Horsepower: 9900 s.h.p. cross-compound steam turbine built by Canadian General Electric Co., Peterborough, Ontario.
Lineage:
- 1967–1972: *Feux-Follets*, Papachristidis Shipping Ltd., Montreal, Quebec
- 1972–2010: *Canadian Leader*, Upper Lakes Shipping, Toronto, Ontario

Notes: Launched at Collingwood Shipyards, Collingwood, Ontario, on June 16, 1967 as Papachristidis Shipping *Feux-Follets*; the last steam-powered laker built. Five remaining vessels in Papachristidis fleet sold to Jackes Shipping, division of Upper Lakes Shipping, on March 16, 1972; *Feux-Follets* became ULS *Canadian Leader*. Laid up at Hamilton, Ontario, July 7, 2009. Towed to International Marine Salvage, Port Colborne, Ontario, for scrap November 2010.

CANADIAN MARINER
- Upper Lakes Shipping, Toronto, Ontario
- Straight-deck bulk carrier

Built: Saint John Shipbuilding & Dry Dock Co., Saint John, New Brunswick, 1963

Length: 730'
Beam: 75'
Depth: 39' 3"
Capacity at mid-summer draft: 27,951 tons
Propulsion: steam turbine
Engine/Horsepower: 9900 s.h.p. cross-compound steam turbine built by Canadian General Electric Co., Peterborough, Ontario
Lineage:
- 1963–1965: *Newbrunswicker*, Calvert Distillers Ltd., Montreal, Quebec, managed by Papachristidis Shipping Ltd.
- 1965–1967: *Newbrunswicker*, Eastern Lake Carriers; Papachristidis management
- 1967–1972: *Grande Hermine*, Eastern Lake Carriers; Papachristidis management
- 1972–present: *Canadian Mariner*, Upper Lakes Shipping, Toronto, Ontario

Notes: Built by Saint John Shipbuilding & Dry Dock Co., Saint John, New Brunswick, for owners Calvert Distillers Ltd., Montreal, Quebec. Launched as *Newbrunswicker* in spring of 1963; chartered to Eastern Lake Carriers and operated under management of Papachristidis Shipping Ltd., Montreal, Quebec. Purchased by Eastern Lake Carriers in 1965 and continued under Papachristidis management. Renamed *Grande Hermine* by Papachristidis in 1967. Sold, along with five other vessels in Papachristidis fleet, to Jackes Shipping, division of Upper Lakes Shipping, on March 16th, 1972. Renamed *Canadian Mariner* by Upper Lakes. Laid-up at Toronto, Ontario, at end of 2002 shipping season; towed to Trois Rivieres, Quebec, July 2004 for use as storage hull.

CANADIAN MINER
- Upper Lakes Shipping, Toronto, Ontario
- Straight-deck bulk carrier

Built: Bow section: George T. Davie & Sons Ltd., Lauzon, Quebec; stern section: Canadian Vickers Ltd., Montreal, Que., 1965
Length: 730' 3"
Beam: 75'
Depth: 39' 1"
Capacity at mid-summer draft: 28,050 tons
Propulsion: diesel
Engines/horsepower: 8000 b.h.p. from four 12-cylinder, 2000-b.h.p Fairbanks-Morse 12-38D 8 1/8 opposed-piston engines built by Canadian Locomotive Co., Kingston, Ontario
Lineage:
- 1965–1988: *Maplecliffe Hall*, Hall Corporation Shipping Ltd. (Halco), Montreal, Quebec
- 1988–1991: *Lemoyne*, Canada Steamship Lines, Montreal, Quebec
- 1994–2011: *Canadian Miner*, Upper Lakes Shipping, Inc., Toronto, Ontario

Notes: Constructed in two sections; bow section built by George T. Davie & Sons Ltd., Lauzon, Quebec; stern section built by Canadian Vickers Ltd., Montreal, Quebec. Sections joined at Champlain Drydock, Lauzon, Quebec. Launched November 13, 1965 at Canadian Vickers in Montreal as Halco *Maplecliffe Hall*. Sold to Canada Steamship Lines in 1988 and renamed *Lemoyne* (second) by CSL. Acquired by Upper Lakes Shipping in 1994 and renamed *Canadian Miner*. Laid up at Toronto, Ontario, 2009–2010. Sold for scrap and renamed m/v *Minor* for scrap tow to Aliaga, Turkey. Departed Montreal, Quebec, in tow on September 14, 2011. Vessel broke from tow line in heavy seas and foundered on rocks on Scatarie Island off Cape Breton, Nova Scotia, September 20, 2011. Hulk broke up on rocks and has not been recovered.

CANADIAN PROVIDER

- Upper Lakes Shipping, Toronto, Ontario
- Straight-deck bulk carrier

Built: Collingwood Shipyards, Collingwood, Ontario, 1963
Length: 730'
Beam: 75'
Depth: 39' 2"
Capacity at mid-summer draft: 27,450 tons
Propulsion: steam turbine
Engine/Horsepower: 9000-s.h.p. steam turbine built by John Inglis Co., Toronto, Ontario
Lineage:
- 1963–1994: *Murray Bay*, Canada Steamship Lines, Montreal, Quebec
- 1994–2011: *Canadian Provider*, Upper Lakes Shipping Ltd., Toronto, Ontario
- 2011–2013: *Algoma Provider*, Algoma Central Corporation, Sault Ste. Marie, Ontario.

Notes: Launched from Collingwood Shipyards, Collingwood, Ontario, on May 3, 1963 as Canada Steamship Lines *Murray Bay* (second). Sold to Upper Lakes Shipping April 8, 1994. Painted in ULS colours and renamed *Canadian Provider* at Toledo, Ohio, in October 1994. Upper Lakes Shipping fleet and ULS interest in Seaway Marine Transport sold to Algoma Central Corporation in 2011. Renamed *Algoma Provider* at Toronto, Ontario, September 9, 2011. Laid up at Montreal, Quebec, December 30, 2012. Sold for scrap in May 2013 and towed to Aliaga, Turkey in June 2013.

CANADIAN TRADER

- Upper Lakes Shipping, Toronto, Ontario
- Straight-deck bulk carrier

Built: Davie Shipbuilding Co., Lauzon, Quebec, 1968
Length: 730'
Beam: 75'
Depth: 39' 8"
Capacity at mid-summer draft: 28,300 tons

Propulsion: diesel
Engines/horsepower: 8310 b.h.p. from three 6-cylinder, 2770-b.h.p Mirrlees Blackstone KMR6 diesels built by Mirrlees Blackstone Ltd., Stockport, England.
Lineage:
- 1968–1983: *Ottercliffe Hall*, Hall Shipping Ltd., Montreal, Quebec
- 1983–1988: *Peter Misener*, Misener Transportation Ltd., St. Catharines, Ontario, under charter from Halco.
- 1988–1994: *David K. Gardiner*, Misener Transportation Ltd., St. Catharines, Ontario
- 1994–2004: *Canadian Trader*, Upper Lakes Shipping, Inc., Toronto, Ontario

Notes: Last conventional Great Lakes straight-decker built. Launched December 12, 1968 as Hall Shipping Ltd. ("Halco"), *Ottercliffe Hall*. Chartered to Misener Transportation Ltd., St. Catharines, Ontario, in August 1983 and named *Royalton*. Halco fleet disbanded in 1987, vessel acquired by Misener Transportation and renamed *Peter Misener* in 1988. Operated by Great Lakes Bulk Carriers 1991–1994; acquired by Upper Lakes Shipping in 1994 and renamed *Canadian Trader*. Laid-up at Toronto, Ontario, December 23, 1999 and served as storage hull at Toronto and later Trois Rivieres, Quebec. Sold for scrap and towed to Alang, India, September 2004.

CANADIAN VENTURE

- Upper Lakes Shipping, Toronto, Ontario
- Straight-deck bulk carrier

Built: Davie Shipbuilding Co., Lauzon, Quebec, 1965
Length: 730' 3"
Beam: 75'
Depth: 39' 2"
Capacity at mid-summer draft: 28,050 tons
Propulsion: diesel
Engines/horsepower: 8000 b.h.p. from four 12-cylinder, 2000-b.h.p Fairbanks-Morse 12-38D 8 1/8 opposed-piston engines built by Canadian Locomotive Co., Kingston, Ontario
Lineage:
- 1965–1988: *Lawrencecliffe Hall* (second), Hall Shipping Ltd., Montreal, Quebec
- 1988–1994: *David K. Gardiner*, Misener Transportation Ltd., St. Catharines, Ontario
- 1994–2004: *Canadian Venture*, Upper Lakes Shipping, Inc., Toronto, Ontario

Notes: Launched April 14, 1965 as Hall Shipping Ltd. ("Halco"), *Lawrencecliffe Hall*. Longest Great Lakes vessel until construction of 1000-foot *Stewart J. Cort* in April 1972. Briefly rated at 9440 b.h.p., as side-drive configuration allowed vessel's two 700-b.h.p. Caterpillar diesels used for electrical power to be employed in tandem with main engines as required for propulsion. Modified to standard configuration and rated at 8000 b.h.p. Rolled on side and sank in St. Lawrence River

after collision with British vessel *Sunek* in snowstorm near Ile D'Orleans, Quebec, November 16, 1965. Righted and re-floated March 16, 1966; repaired and returned to service August 1966. Halco fleet disbanded in 1987, vessel acquired by Misener Transportation and renamed *David K. Gardiner* in 1988. Operated by Great Lakes Bulk Carriers 1991–1994; acquired by Upper Lakes Shipping in 1994 and renamed *Canadian Venture*. Laid-up at Toronto, Ontario, December 2001; sold for scrap and towed to Alang, India, September 2004.

CANADIAN VOYAGER

- Upper Lakes Shipping, Toronto, Ontario
- Straight-deck bulk carrier

Built: Collingwood Shipyards, Collingwood, Ontario, 1963
Length: 730'
Beam: 75'
Depth: 39' 2"
Capacity at mid-summer draft: 27,050 tons
Propulsion: steam turbine
Engine/Horsepower: 9000 s.h.p., cross-compound, steam turbine built by Canadian General Electric Co., Peterborough, Ontario
Lineage:
- 1963–1964: *Black Bay*, Owned by Canadian General Electric, managed by Canada Steamship Lines, Montreal, Quebec
- 1964–1994: *Black Bay*, Canada Steamship Lines, Montreal, Quebec
- 1994–2002: *Canadian Voyager*, Upper Lakes Shipping, Inc., Toronto, Ontario

Notes: Launched as *Black Bay* at Collingwood Shipyards, Collingwood, Ontario, on September 20, 1963; owned by Canadian General Electric Co., operated by Canada Steamship Lines. Title for vessel passed to Canada Steamship Lines in 1964. Sold to Upper Lakes Shipping Ltd., Toronto, Ontario, in 1994 and renamed *Canadian Voyager*. Laid-up at Montreal, Quebec, December 23, 2001; sold for scrap and towed to Aliaga, Turkey, August 2002.

PHILIP R. CLARKE

- Great Lakes Fleet, Inc., Duluth, Minnesota
- Self-unloader; conversion from straight-deck bulk carrier

Built: American Ship Building Co., Lorain, Ohio, 1952
Length: 767' (lengthened from 647')
Beam: 70'
Depth: 36'
Capacity at mid-summer draft: 25,300 tons
Propulsion: steam turbine
Engine/Horsepower: 7700 s.h.p. steam turbine built by Westinghouse Electric Corporation, Philadelphia, Pennsylvania
Lineage:
- 1952–1981: *Philip R. Clarke*, Pittsburgh Steamship Co., Cleveland, Ohio

Detail, *John Sherwin*, August 2006.

- 1981–2004: *Philip R. Clarke*, USS Great Lakes Fleet, Cleveland, Ohio
- 2004–present: *Philip R. Clarke*, CN-Great Lakes Fleet Inc., operated by Keystone Shipping Co., Bala Cynwyd, Pennsylvania

Notes: Constructed in 1952 by American Ship Building Co., at Lorain, Ohio, as *Philip R. Clarke* for U.S. Steel's Pittsburgh Steamship Co. Lengthened by 120 feet by Fraser Shipyards, Superior, Wisconsin, during winter lay-up 1974–75. Converted to self-unloader at Fraser Shipyards during winter lay-up 1981–82. Canadian National Railway acquired USS Great Lakes Fleet in 2004; fleet operated by Keystone Shipping Co., Bala Cynwyd, Pennsylvania.

CUYAHOGA

- Lower Lakes Towing Co., Port Dover, Ontario
- Self-unloader; conversion from straight-deck bulk carrier

Built: American Ship Building Co., Lorain, Ohio, 1943
Length: 620'
Beam: 60'
Depth: 35'
Capacity at mid-summer draft: 15,675 tons (reduced from 16,300 tons in conversion to self-unloader)
Propulsion — as built: steam

Propulsion — current: diesel
Engine/horsepower — original: American Steamship Co., 2500 i.h.p., tandem compound, 2-cylinder Lentz Standard Marine Engine
Engine/horsepower — current: Caterpillar 3608-series, 8-cylinder, 3084 b.h.p., installed 2000
Lineage:
- 1943–1957: *J. Burton Ayers*, Great Lakes Steamship Co.
- 1957–1966: *J. Burton Ayers*, Northwestern Mutual Life Insurance Co., vessel managed by Wilson Marine Transit Co.
- 1966–1972: *J. Burton Ayers*, Wilson Marine Transit Co.
- 1972–1974: *J. Burton Ayers*, Kinsman Marine Transport Co.
- 1974–1994: *J. Burton Ayers*, Columbia Transportation Division, Oglebay Norton Co., Cleveland, Ohio
- 1994–1995: *J. Burton Ayers*, Oglebay Norton Co., Cleveland, Ohio
- 1995–present: *Cuyahoga*, Lower Lakes Towing, Co., Port Dover, Ontario

Notes: Maritime class L6-S-A1, constructed in 1943 by American Ship Building Co., Lorain, Ohio, as *Mesabi* for United States Maritime Commission. Delivered to Great Lakes Steamship Co., Cleveland, Ohio, upon completion and christened *J. Burton Ayers*. Retained name through various ownerships. Converted to self-unloader by American Ship Building, Toledo, Ohio, 1974.

Boilers converted from coal-to oil-fired 1975. Laid-up at Toledo, Ohio, December 1990. De-commissioned August 15, 1991. Sold to Lower Lakes Towing Co., August 1, 1995. Christened *Cuyahoga* at Sarnia, Ontario, November 1995. Converted to diesel at Sarnia, Ontario, winter 2000.

JOSEPH H. FRANTZ

- Oglebay Norton Marine Services, under charter to Great Lakes Associates (Kinsman)
- Self-unloader; conversion from straight-deck bulk carrier

Built: Great Lakes Engineering Works, River Rouge, Michigan, 1925
Length: 618'
Beam: 62'
Depth: 32'
Capacity at mid-summer draft: 13,600 tons
Propulsion — as built: steam
Propulsion — final: diesel
Engine/horsepower — original: 2500-i.h.p. triple expansion steam engine built by Great Lakes Engineering Works, River Rouge, Michigan
Engine/horsepower — second: 5323-i.h.p., 5-cylinder Skinner Marine Unaflow reciprocating steam engine from Skinner Engine Co., Erie, Pennsylvania
Engine/Horsepower — final: 4000 b.h.p., 12-cylinder DMRV-12-4 Enterprise engine from by General Metals, San Francisco, California
Lineage:
- 1924–1944: *Joseph H. Frantz*, Columbia Steamship. Co., Cleveland, Ohio
- 1944–2003: *Joseph H. Frantz*, Oglebay Norton Co., Cleveland, Ohio
- 2003–2004: *Joseph H. Frantz*, Oglebay Norton Co., Cleveland, Ohio, chartered to Great Lakes Associates (Kinsman)

Notes: First vessel built by Great Lakes Engineering Works, River Rouge, Michigan. Launched on October 18, 1924 as Columbia Steamship. Co., as *Joseph H. Frantz*. Columbia fleet transferred to Oglebay Norton in 1944. Original 2500-i.h.p. triple expansion steam engine replaced with 5323-i.h.p., 5-cylinder Skinner Marine Unaflow from Skinner Engine Co., Erie, Pennsylvania, in 1955. Modifications at Christy Corporation, Sturgeon Bay, Wisconsin, during winter of 1965 included conversion to self-unloader and dieselization with 12-cylinder DMRV-12-4 Enterprise engine from by General Metals, San Francisco, California. Oglebay Norton chartered *Frantz* to chartered to Great Lakes Associates (Kinsman) in 2003. Vessel given Kinsman stack colours and traditional "S" on stack. Laid-up at Buffalo, New York, December 16, 2004; towed to International Marine Salvage, Port Colborne, Ontario, for scrap April 29, 2005.

FRONTENAC

- Canada Steamship Lines, Montreal, Quebec
- Self-unloader; conversion from straight-deck bulk carrier

Built: Davie Shipbuilding Ltd., Lauzon, Quebec, 1968
Length: 729' 10"
Beam: 75' 4"
Depth: 39' 8"
Capacity at mid-summer draft: 26,822 tons
Propulsion: diesel
Engine/Horsepower: 9600 b.h.p., 6-cylinder Sulzer 6RND76
Lineage:
• 1967–present: *Frontenac* (fifth), Canada Steamship Lines, Montreal, Quebec
Notes: Fifth Canada Steamship Lines vessel to carry the name *Frontenac*. Launched at Davie Shipbuilding, Lauzon, Quebec, December 12, 1967. Converted to self-unloader during winter 1972–73 at Collingwood Shipyards, Collingwood, Ontario.

EDWIN H. GOTT
• Great Lakes Fleet, Inc., Duluth, Minnesota
• Self-unloader
Built: Bay Shipbuilding Corp., Sturgeon Bay, Wisconsin, 1979
Length: 1004'
Beam: 105'
Depth: 52'
Capacity at mid-summer draft: 74,100 tons
Propulsion: diesel
Engines/horsepower: 19, 500 b.h.p. from two 16-cylinder, 9750-b.h.p. diesels built by DeLaval Turbine Inc., Enterprise Division, Oakland, California.
Lineage:
• 1979–2004: *Edwin H. Gott*, United States Steel Corp., Great Lakes Fleet
• 2004–present: *Edwin H. Gott*, CN-Great Lakes Fleet Inc., operated by Keystone Shipping Co., Bala Cynwyd, Pennsylvania
Notes: *Edwin H. Gott* launched at Bay Shipbuilding, Sturgeon Bay, Wisconsin, July 19, 1978; eighth of 13 1000-foot "super carriers" built for service on the Great Lakes between 1972 and 1981. Vessel employed almost exclusively in taconite trade from Lake Superior ports to Gary and Indiana Harbor, Indiana as well as Ohio ports of Conneaut and Lorain. Canadian National Railway acquired USS Great Lakes Fleet in 2004; fleet operated by Keystone Shipping Co., Bala Cynwyd, Pennsylvania.

HALIFAX
• Canada Steamship Lines, Montreal, Quebec
• Self-unloader; conversion from straight-deck bulk carrier
Built: Davie Shipbuilding Ltd., Lauzon, Quebec 1963
Length: 730' 2"
Beam: 75'
Depth: 39' 3"
Capacity at mid-summer draft: 30,100 tons
Propulsion: steam turbine

Engine/Horsepower: 9000-s.h.p. steam turbine built by John Inglis Co., Toronto, Ontario
Lineage:
• 1963–1988: *Frankcliffe Hall*, Hall Corporation Shipping Ltd. (Halco), Montreal, Quebec
• 1988–2011: *Halifax*, Canada Steamship Lines, Montreal, Quebec
Notes: Launched December 17, 1962 by Davie Shipbuilding, Lauzon, Quebec, as Halco *Frankcliffe Hall*. Converted to self-unloader at Port Arthur Shipbuilding Co., Thunder Bay, Ontario, during winter 1979–80. Sold to Canada Steamship Lines in 1988 and renamed *Halifax*. Laid up at Montreal December 28, 2008 and idle until retired in 2011. Sold for scrap and towed to Aliaga, Turkey in May 2011.

ELTON HOYT 2ND — see Michipicoten.

J.A.W. IGLEHART
• Inland Lakes Management, Alpena, Michigan
• Cement carrier
Built: Sun Shipbuilding and Dry Dock Co., Chester, Pennsylvania, 1936
Length: 501' 6"
Beam: 68' 3"
Depth: 37'
Capacity at mid-summer draft: 12,500 tons
Propulsion: steam turbine
Engine/Horsepower: 4400 s.h.p., DeLaval cross-compound steam turbine built by Transamerica DeLaval Inc., Turbine and Compressor Division, Trenton, New Jersey.
Lineage:
• 1936–1943: *Pan-Amoco*, Pan-American Petroleum and Transportation Co., New York, New York
• 1943–1955: *Pan-Amoco*, American Oil Co., Baltimore, Maryland
• 1955–1959: *Amoco*, American Oil Co., Baltimore, Maryland
• 1960–1964: *H.R. Schemm*, Huron Portland Cement Co., Alpena, Michigan
• 1964–1988: *J.A.W. Iglehart*, Huron Portland Cement Co., Alpena, Michigan
• 1988–present: *J.A.W. Iglehart*, Inland Lakes Management, Alpena, Michigan
Notes: Constructed in 1936 by Sun Shipbuilding and Dry Dock Co., Chester, Pennsylvania, as Pan-American Petroleum and Transportation Co., ocean-going tanker *Pan-Amoco*. Sold to American Oil Co., Baltimore, Maryland, in 1943; name shortened to *Amoco* in 1955. Sold for scrap 1959–1960; hull purchased by Huron Portland Cement, Alpena, Michigan, for conversion to cement carrier. Towed to Sturgeon Bay, Wisconsin, for rebuilding and renamed *H.R. Schemm*. Work not performed and vessel never sailed under this name. Relocated in 1964

to American Ship Building Co., Chicago, Illinois, and converted to cement carrier. Christened *J.A.W. Iglehart*, May 26, 1965; ranked as largest self-unloading cement carrier in the world. Vessel transferred to Inland Lakes Management. Laid-up at Superior, Wisconsin, November 5, 2006. Moved to LaFarge Cement to replace J.B. Ford as storage hull.

HERBERT C. JACKSON
• Interlake Steamship Co., Richfield, Ohio
• Self-unloader; conversion from straight-deck bulk carrier
Built: Great Lakes Engineering Works, River Rouge, Michigan, 1959
Length: 690'
Beam: 75'
Depth: 37' 6"
Capacity at mid-summer draft: 24,800 tons
Propulsion: steam turbine
Engine/Horsepower: 6600 s.h.p., cross-compound, steam turbine built by General Electric Co., Lynn, Massachusetts
Lineage:
• 1959–2006: *Herbert C. Jackson*, Interlake Steamship Co., Richfield, Ohio
Notes: Constructed at Great Lakes Engineering Works, River Rouge, Michigan, as Interlake Steamship Co., *Herbert C. Jackson*. Placed in service May 14, 1959; second last vessel to be completed by River Rouge yards. Modifications made at Defoe Shipbuilding, Bay City, Michigan, during winter lay-up 1974–75 included conversion to self-unloader and modifying boilers from coal-fired to oil-burning operation.

KINSMAN INDEPENDENT — see Ojibway

GORDON C. LEITCH
• Upper Lakes Shipping, Toronto, Ontario
• Self-unloader
Built: Canadian Vickers Shipyard, Montreal, Quebec, 1968
Length: 730'
Beam: 75'
Depth: 42'
Capacity at mid-summer draft: 31,668 tons
Propulsion: diesel
Engine/Horsepower: 9600 b.h.p., 6-cylinder Sulzer 6RND76 engine built by Scotts' Shipbuilding & Engine Co., Ltd., Greenock, Scotland
Lineage:
• 1968–1994: *Ralph Misner,* Scott Misener Steamships Ltd., St, Catharines, Ontario
• 1994–2011: *Gordon C. Leitch*, Upper Lakes Shipping Co., Toronto, Ontario
• 2011–2012; *Gordon C. Leitch*, Algoma Central Corporation, Sault Ste. Marie, Ontario

- 2011–present: Algoma Central Corporation, Sault Ste. Marie, Ontario

Notes:
Built by Canadian Vickers Shipyard, Montreal, Quebec; christened Ralph Misener on June 1, 1968. Acquired by Upper Lakes Shipping in 1994 and renamed *Gordon C. Leitch*. Upper Lakes Shipping fleet and ULS interest in Seaway Marine Transport sold to Algoma Central Corporation in 2011. Vessel retained name under *Algoma flag*. Winter layup at Montreal, Quebec, December 28, 2011. Sold for scrap in June 2012 and towed to Aliaga, Turkey, departing Montreal on August 15.

JOHN D. LEITCH
- Upper Lakes Shipping, Toronto, Ontario
- Self-unloader

Built: Port Weller Dry Docks, St. Catharines, Ontario, 1967
Length: 730'
Beam: 75'
Depth: 45'
Capacity at mid-summer draft: 31,600 tons
Propulsion: diesel
Engine/Horsepower: 7394 b.h.p., 5-cylinder Burmeister & Wain 5-74-VT2BF -160 engine built by Harland & Wolff Ltd., Belfast, Northern Ireland
Lineage:
- 1967–2002: *Canadian Century*, Upper Lakes Shipping Co., Toronto, Ontario
- 2002–2011: *John D. Leitch*, Upper Lakes Shipping Co., Toronto, Ontario

Notes: Built by Port Weller Dry Docks, St. Catharines, Ontario, in 1967; christened Upper Lakes Shipping *Canadian Century* April 15, 1967. Extensive refit at Port Weller during winter of 2002 included replacement of mid-section, including cargo holds and self-unloading equipment. Renamed *John D. Leitch* and returned to work in May 2002. Upper Lakes Shipping fleet and ULS interest in Seaway Marine Transport sold to Algoma Central Corporation in 2011. Vessel retained name under *Algoma flag*.

MANISTEE
- Grand River Navigation/Lower Lakes Transportation Co., Cleveland, Ohio
- Self-unloader; conversion from straight-deck bulk carrier

Built: Great Lakes Engineering Works, River Rouge, Michigan, 1943
Length: 620' 6"
Beam: 60' 3"
Depth: 35'
Capacity at mid-summer draft: 14,900 tons
Propulsion — as built: steam
Propulsion — current: diesel

Engine/Horsepower — original: 2500-i.h.p. triple expansion steam engine built by Great Lakes Engineering Works, River Rouge, Michigan
Engine/Horsepower — current: 2950-b.h.p. 20-cyliner Electro-Motive 645E6
Lineage:
- 1943–1986: *Richard J. Reiss*, Reiss Steamship Co., Sheboygan, Wisconsin
- 1986–1992: *Richard J. Reiss*, American Steamship Co., Williamsville, New York
- 1992–2004: *Richard Reiss*, Erie Sand Steamship Co., Erie, Pennsylvania
- 2004–2005: *Richard Reiss*, Grand River Navigation/Lower Lakes Transportation Co., Cleveland, Ohio
- 2005–present: *Manistee*, Grand River Navigation/Lower Lakes Transportation Co., Cleveland, Ohio

Notes: Maritime class L6-S-B1, constructed in 1943 by Great Lakes Engineering Works, River Rouge, Michigan, as *Adirondack* for United States Maritime Commission. Renamed *Richard J. Reiss* (second) upon delivery to Reiss Steamship Co., at Sheboygan, Wisconsin, May 28, 1943. Converted to self-unloader in 1964. Dieselized in 1976 with 2950-h.p. Electro-Motive 645-series engine. C. Reiss Coal Co., parent of Reiss Steamship, sold fleet to American Steamship Co., in 1969. Reiss fleet continued to operate separately until formally merged into American Steamship Co., on July 23, 1986. Chartered by Erie Sand Steamship Co., Erie, Pennsylvania, in 1986; name shortened to *Richard Reiss*. Laid-up for winter at Erie, Pa., December 18, 2001; Erie Sand Steamship Co., and parent Erie Sand & Gravel Co., purchased by Oglebay Norton in January 2002. Vessel remained in lay-up until sale to Lower Lakes Transportation's Grand River Navigation Co., in January 2004. Sailed for 2004 season as Grand River Navigation Co., *Richard Reiss* with stack colours changed to those of Lower Lakes. Vessel painted to Lower Lakes colours during five-year inspection at Bayship, Sturgeon Bay, Wisconsin, December 2004. Christened Grand River Navigation Co., *Manistee* at Sarnia, Ontario, March 14, 2005.

MANTADOC — see Maritime Trader

MAPLEGLEN
- Canada Steamship Lines, Montreal, Quebec
- Straight-deck bulk carrier

Built: Collingwood Shipyards, Collingwood, Ontario, 1960
Length: 715' 3"
Beam: 75'
Depth: 37' 9"
Capacity at mid-summer draft: 26,100 tons
Propulsion: steam turbine
Engine/Horsepower: 9350 s.h.p., cross-compound, steam turbine built by General Electric Co., Lynn, Massachusetts

Lineage:
- 1960–1986: *Carol Lake*, Carryore Ltd., Montreal, Quebec
- 1986–1987: *Carol Lake*, Algoma Central Corp., Sault Ste. Marie, Ontario
- 1987–1994: *Algocape* (first), Algoma Central Corp., Sault Ste. Marie, Ontario
- 1994–2001: *Mapleglen*, P&H Shipping (Parrish & Heimbecker), Mississauga, Ontario
- 2001–2003: *Mapleglen*, Canada Steamship Lines, Montreal, Quebec

Notes: Launched from Collingwood Shipyards, Collingwood, Ontario, as Carryore Ltd., *Carol Lake*, on May 5, 1960. Sold to Algoma Central in 1986 after breakup of Carryore fleet. Renamed Algoma Central *Algocape* (first) in 1987. Sold to P&H Shipping in 1994 and named *Mapleglen*. Retained *Mapleglen* name when last two active vessels in P&H fleet sold to Canada Steamship Lines in July 2001. Sold for scrap and towed to Alang, India, September 2003.

MARITIME TRADER
- Voyageur Maritime Trading, Ridgeville, Ontario
- Straight deck bulk carrier

Built: Collingwood Shipyards Ltd., Collingwood, Ontario, 1966
Length: 607' 10"
Beam: 62'
Depth: 36'
Capacity at mid-summer draft: 19,093 tons
Propulsion: diesel
Engines/Horsepower: 5332 b.h.p. from four 8-cylinder, 1333-b.h.p. Fairbanks-Morse 8-38D 8 1/8 opposed-piston engines built by Canadian Locomotive Co., Kingston, Ontario
Lineage:
- 1966–2002: *Mantadoc*, N.M. Paterson & Sons Ltd., Thunder Bay, Ontario.
- 2002–2004: *Teakglen*, Canada Steamship Lines, Montreal, Quebec
- 2004–2005: *Teakglen* (storage hull), Goderich Elevators Ltd., Goderich, Ontario
- 2005–2011: *Maritime Trader*, Voyageur Marine Transport Ltd., Ridgeville, Ontario
- 2011–present: *Manitoba*, Lower Lakes Towing, Co., Port Dover, Ontario

Notes: N.M. Paterson & Sons Mantadoc launched at Collingwood Shipyards November 23, 1966. Paterson fleet, reduced to just three operating vessels, sold to Canada Steamship Lines March 21, 2002. *Mantadoc* renamed CSL *Teakglen*, but saw little service in 2002; contracted to Goderich Elevators, Goderich, Ontario, in fall 2002 for use as storage vessel. Title transferred to Goderich Elevators by January 2004. Vessel sold to Wayne Elliot by summer 2005 and towed to Thunder Bay for refit under Voyageur Maritime

Detail, *James Norris*, October 2006.

Trading Inc., in September. Rechristened *Maritime Trader* at Thunder Bay September 30, 2005 and returned to service under management of Voyageur Marine Transport, Ridgeville, Ontario. Purchased by Lower Lakes Towing July 2011 and christened Manitoba.

MAUMEE
- Grand River Navigation/Lower Lakes Transportation Co., Cleveland, Ohio
- Self-unloader; conversion from straight-deck bulk carrier

Built: American Ship Building Co., Lorain, Ohio, 1929
Length: 604' 9"
Beam: 60'
Depth: 32'
Capacity at mid-summer draft: 12,650 tons
Propulsion — as built: steam
Propulsion — current: diesel
Engine/Horsepower — original: 2200 i.h.p., triple-expansion steam engine, American Ship Building Co., Lorain, Ohio
Engine/Horsepower — current: 3240 b.h.p., 12-cylinder Nordberg FS-1312-H5C built by Nordberg Manufacturing Co., Milwaukee, Wisconsin
Lineage:
- 1929–1960: *William G. Clyde*, Pittsburgh Steamship Co., Cleveland, Ohio

- 1960–1967: *Calcite II*, Bradley Transportation Co., Rogers City, Michigan, managed by Pittsburgh Steamship
- 1967–1981: *Calcite II*, Pittsburgh Steamship Co., Cleveland, Ohio
- 1981–2001: *Calcite II*, USS Great Lakes Fleet, Cleveland, Ohio
- 2001–2011: *Maumee*, Grand River Navigation/Lower Lakes Transportation Co., Cleveland, Ohio

Notes: Constructed in 1929 by American Ship Building Co., as *William G. Clyde* for U.S. Steel's Pittsburgh Steamship Co., Cleveland Ohio. Reassigned to Pittsburgh Steamship-managed Bradley Transportation Co., Rogers City, Michigan, in 1960. Converted to self-unloader during winter of 1960–61 by Manitowoc Shipbuilding Co., Manitowoc, Wisconsin. Dieselized in 1964 with 12-cylinder engine built by Nordberg Manufacturing Co., Milwaukee, Wisconsin. Returned to Pittsburgh Steamship Co., with merger of U.S. Steel-owned Bradley and Pittsburgh fleets July 1, 1967. Re-flagged under USS Great Lakes Fleet created in June 1981. Laid-up at Sarnia, Ontario, December, 2000, in anticipation of sale to U.S. subsidiary of Lower Lakes Towing. Sold with fleet mates *Myron C. Taylor* and *George A. Sloan* to Lower Lakes affiliate Grand River Navigation Co., Cleveland, Ohio, March 2001. Christened *Maumee* at Sarnia, April 21, 2001. Laid up at Cleveland, Ohio, in late 2010. Towed to International Marine and Salvage, Port Colborne, Ontario, for scrap in December 2011.

MICHIPICOTEN
- Lower Lakes Towing Co., Port Dover, Ontario
- Self-unloader; conversion from straight-deck bulk carrier

Built: Bethlehem Shipbuilding & Drydock Co., Sparrows Point, Maryland, 1952
Length: 689' 6"
Beam: 70'
Depth: 37'
Capacity at mid-summer draft: 22,300 tons
Propulsion: diesel
Engine/Horsepower: Engine/horsepower — as built: 7700 s.h.p., cross-compound steam turbine built by Bethlehem Steel Co.
Engine/horsepower — current: 8160 b.h.p., 6-cylinder MaK 6M32C
Lineage:
- 1952–2003: *Elton Hoyt 2nd*, Interlake Steamship Co., Richfield, Ohio
- 2003–2011: *Michipicoten*, Lower Lakes Towing, Co., Port Dover, Ontario

Notes: Constructed by Bethlehem Shipbuilding & Drydock Co., Sparrows Point, Maryland, in 1952. Built off-lakes due to backlog of orders at Great Lakes builders. Towed via New Orleans and Mississippi and Illinois Rivers to Chicago for completion. Lengthened by 72 feet in 1957. Converted to self-unloader by American Ship building, Toledo, Ohio, in 1980. Laid-up at Superior, Wisconsin, in fall 2001 and did not sail until after purchase by Lower Lakes Towing Co., in April 2003. Christened Lower lakes Towing *Michipicoten* at Sarnia, Ontario, on May 24, 2003 and sailed for Marquette, Michigan, on maiden voyage on June 13, 2003. Conversion from steam to diesel carried out at Sarnia, Ontario, December 2010-May 2011.

MIDDLETOWN — see American Victory

MISSISSAGI
- Lower Lakes Towing Co., Port Dover, Ontario
- Self-unloader; conversion from straight-deck bulk carrier

Built: Great Lakes Engineering Works, River Rouge, Michigan, 1943
Length: 620' 6"
Beam: 60'
Depth: 35'
Capacity at mid-summer draft: 15,800 tons
Propulsion — as built: steam
Propulsion — current: diesel
Engine/Horsepower — original: 2500-i.h.p. triple expansion steam engine built by Great Lakes Engineering Works, River Rouge, Michigan
Engine/Horsepower — current: 4500 b.h.p., 12-cylinder Caterpillar 3612TA

Detail, "Still Steamin," *St. Marys Challenger,* September 2006.

Lineage:

- 1943–1966: *George A. Sloan*, Pittsburgh Steamship Co., Cleveland, Ohio
- 1966–1967: *George A. Sloan*, Bradley Transportation Co., Rogers City, Michigan, managed by Pittsburgh Steamship
- 1967–1981: *George A. Sloan*, Pittsburgh Steamship Co., Cleveland, Ohio
- 1981–2001: *George A. Sloan,* USS Great Lakes Fleet, Cleveland, Ohio
- 2001–present: *Mississagi*, Lower Lakes Towing Co., Port Dover, Ontario

Notes: Maritime class L6-S-B1, constructed in 1943 by Great Lakes Engineering Works, River Rouge, Michigan, as *Hill Annex* for United States Maritime Commission. Delivered to Pittsburgh Steamship Co., Cleveland, Ohio, upon completion July 22, 1943 and christened *George A. Sloan*. Suffered structural cracks in encounter with moderate swells on Lake Huron September 1943 and returned for hull strengthening. Sold to Bradley Transportation Co., Rogers City, Michigan, in 1966. Converted to self-unloader at Fraser Shipyards, Superior, Wisconsin, in winter of 1965–66 and renamed *George A. Sloan*. Returned to Pittsburgh Steamship Co., with merger of U.S. Steel-owned Bradley and Pittsburgh fleets July 1, 1967. Re-flagged under USS Great Lakes Fleet created in June 1981.

Dieselized during winter lay-up in 1984–85 with installation of 4,500 b.h.p., 12-cylinder Caterpillar 3612TA. Laid-up at Sarnia, Ontario, December, 2000, in anticipation of sale to Lower Lakes Towing. Sold with fleet mates *Myron C. Taylor* and *Calcite II* to Lower Lakes and Lower Lakes affiliate Grand River Navigation Co., Cleveland, Ohio, March 2001. Given Canadian registry and christened Lower Lakes Towing *Mississagi* at Sarnia, April 21, 2001.

MONTREALAIS

- Upper Lakes Shipping, Toronto, Ontario
- Straight-deck bulk carrier

Built: Bow section: George T. Davie & Sons Ltd., Lauzon, Quebec; stern section: Canadian Vickers Ltd., Montreal, Que., 1962
Length: 730'
Beam: 75'
Depth: 39'
Capacity at mid-summer draft: 28,443 tons
Propulsion: steam turbine
Engine/Horsepower: 9900 s.h.p., cross-compound, MD70 steam turbine built by Canadian General Electric Co., Peterborough, Ontario

Lineage:

- 1962–1965: *Montrealais*, Canadian Vickers Ltd., Montreal,

Quebec. Chartered to Papachristidis Co., Montreal, Quebec
- 1965–1972: *Montrealais*, Eastern Lake Carriers, Montreal, Quebec, managed by Papachristidis Co., Montreal, Quebec
- 1972–2011: *Montrealais*, Upper Lakes Shipping Co., Toronto, Ontario
- 2012–present: *Algoma Montrealais,* Algoma Central Corporation, Sault Ste. Marie, Ontario

Notes: Ordered by Papachristidis Co., Montreal, Quebec as *Montrealer*, name changed to *Montrealais* prior to completion. Constructed in two sections; bow section built by George T. Davie & Sons Ltd., Lauzon, Quebec; stern section built by Canadian Vickers Ltd., Montreal, Quebec. Sections joined at Champlain Drydock, Lauzon, Quebec. Christened *Montrealais* at Canadian Vickers in Montreal on April 12, 1962. Title to vessel held by Canadian Vickers; chartered to Papachristidis Co., from 1962 to 1965. Purchased by Eastern Lake Carriers in 1965 and continued under Papachristidis management. Sold to Upper Lakes Shipping in 1972.

JAMES NORRIS

- Upper Lakes Shipping, Toronto, Ontario
- Self-unloader; conversion from straight-deck bulk carrier

Built: Midland Shipbuilding Co., Midland, Ontario, 1952
Length: 663' 6"
Beam: 67'
Depth: 35'
Capacity at mid-summer draft: 18,600 tons
Propulsion: steam
Engine/Horsepower: 4440 i.h.p., 5-cylinder Vickers-Skinner Unaflow reciprocating steam engine built by Canadian Vickers Ltd., Montreal, Quebec

Lineage:

- 1952–2011: *James Norris*, Upper Lakes and St. Lawrence Transportation Co., Toronto, Ontario

Notes: Christened Upper Lakes and St. Lawrence Transportation Co., *James Norris* at Midland Shipbuilding Co., Midland, Ontario, December 10, 1951, by Mr. and Mrs. James Norris. Converted to self-unloader at Port Weller Dry Docks, St. Catharines, Ontario, during winter lay-up 1980–81. Oldest Canadian-built, steam-powered lake boat in service until laid up at Port Colborne, Ontario, December 6, 2011. Moved to International Marine Salvage, Port Colborne, for scrap December 9, 2011.

OAKGLEN

- Canada Steamship Lines, Montreal, Quebec
- Straight-deck bulk carrier

Built: Midland Shipyards, Midland, Ontario, 1954
Length: 714' 6"
Beam: 70' 3"
Depth: 37' 3"
Capacity at mid-summer draft: 22,950 tons
Propulsion: steam turbine

Engine/Horsepower: 8500 s.h.p., cross-compound, steam turbine built by Westinghouse Electric Corp., Sunnyvale, California
Lineage:
- 1954–1990: *T.R. McLagan*, Canada Steamship Lines, Montreal, Quebec
- 1990–2001: *Oakglen*, P&H Shipping (Parrish & Heimbecker), Mississauga, Ontario
- 2001–2003: *Oakglen*, Canada Steamship Lines, Montreal, Quebec

Notes: Last vessel built by Midland Shipyards, Midland, Ontario. Launched at Midland on November 7, 1953 as Canada Steamship Lines *T.R. McLagan*. Embarked on maiden voyage on April 25, 1954, bound for Superior, Wisconsin to load iron ore for Hamilton, Ontario. Laid-up by CSL at Kingston, Ontario, in 1984; transferred to Toronto for use as storage hull in 1987. Refit at Port Weller Dry Docks, St. Catharines, Ontario, in 1988 and chartered to P&H Shipping, Mississauga, Ontario. Sold to P&H in 1990 and christened *Oakglen*. Returned to Canada Steamship Lines fold and retained *Oakglen* name when last two active vessels in P&H fleet sold to CSL in July 2001. Laid-up at Montreal, Quebec, in December 2002. Sold for scrap and towed to Alang, India, for scrap in October 2003.

OJIBWAY
- Lower Lakes Towing, Co., Port Dover, Ontario
- Straight-deck bulk carrier

Built: Defoe Shipbuilding, Bay City Michigan, 1952
Length: 642' 3"
Beam: 67'
Depth: 35'
Capacity at mid-summer draft: 20,668 tons
Propulsion — as built: steam turbine
Propulsion — current: diesel
Engine/Horsepower — original: 4400-s.h.p. steam turbine built by Bethlehem Steel Co., Shipbuilding Division, Quincy, Massachusetts.
Engine/Horsepower — current: 4100 b.h.p., 16-cylinder General Electric 7FDM EFI engine
Lineage:
- 1952–1962: *Charles L. Hutchinson*, Pioneer Steamship Co., Cleveland, Ohio
- 1962–1988: *Ernest R. Breech*, Ford Motor Co.
- 1988–2004: *Kinsman Independent*, Kinsman Lines, Inc.
- 2005–2007: *Voyageur Independent*, Voyageur Marine Transport, Ridgeville, Ontario
- 2007–present: *Ojibway,* Lower Lakes Towing, Co., Port Dover, Ontario

Notes:
Built by Defoe Shipbuilding, Bay City Michigan, in 1952 as Pioneer Steamship Co., *Charles L. Hutchinson*. Powered by 4400-s.h.p Bethlehem Steel Corp., steam turbine recovered

from vessel *Alcoa Protector,* sunk by Japanese during World War II. Purchased by Ford Motor Co., following dissolution of Pioneer fleet in 1961. Sold to Kinsman Lines in 1988 and named *Kinsman Independent*. Last straight-decker to deliver grain to General Mills elevator in Buffalo, New York. Laid-up at Buffalo December 16, 2002. Sold to McKeil Work Boats, Ltd., Hamilton, Ontario, September 2004. Sold to Voyageur Marine Transport, vessel dieselized and refit by McKeil and returned to service as *Voyageur Independent* in November 2005. Purchased by Lower Lakes Towing in 2007 and christened *Ojibway* in 2008.

HON. JAMES L. OBERSTAR — see Charles M. Beeghly

QUEBECOIS
- Upper Lakes Shipping, Toronto, Ontario
- Straight-deck bulk carrier

Built: Canadian Vickers Shipyards, Montreal, Quebec, 1963
Length: 730'
Beam: 75'
Depth: 39'
Capacity at mid-summer draft: 27,800 tons
Propulsion: steam turbine
Engine/Horsepower: 9896 s.h.p. MD70 steam turbine built by Canadian General Electric Co., Peterborough, Ontario
Lineage:
- 1967–1972: *Quebecois*, Papachristidis Shipping Ltd., Montreal, Quebec
- 1972–2012: *Quebecois*, Upper Lakes Shipping, Toronto, Ontario
- 2012–2013: *Algoma Quebecois*, Algoma Central Corporation, Sault Ste. Marie, Ontario

Notes: Launched in 1963 as Papachristidis Shipping *Quebecois*. Five remaining vessels in Papachristidis fleet sold to Jackes Shipping, division of Upper Lakes Shipping, on March 16th, 1972. Vessel continued to sail as *Quebecois* under Upper Lakes flag. Upper Lakes Shipping fleet and ULS interest in Seaway Marine Transport sold to Algoma Central Corporation in 2011. Renamed *Algoma Quebecois* in 2012. Towed to International Marine Salvage, Port Colborne, for scrap in November 2013.

RICHARD REISS — see Manistee

RESERVE
- Oglebay—Norton Co., Cleveland, Ohio
- Self-unloader; conversion from straight-deck bulk carrier

Built: Great Lakes Engineering Works, River Rouge, Michigan, 1953
Length: 767'
Beam: 70'

Depth: 36'
Capacity at mid-summer draft: 25,500 tons
Propulsion: steam turbine
Engine/Horsepower: 7700 s.h.p. steam turbine built by Westinghouse Electric Corporation, Philadelphia, Pennsylvania
Lineage:
- 1953–1994: *Reserve*, Columbia Transportation Division, Oglebay Norton Co., Cleveland, Ohio
- 1994–2006: *Reserve*, Oglebay Norton Co., Cleveland, Ohio

Notes: Constructed at Great Lakes Engineering Works, River Rouge, Michigan, as Columbia Transportation Division, Oglebay Norton Co., *Reserve*. Lengthened by 120 feet in 1975 and converted to self-unloader in 1983. Sold to K&K Warehousing Inc., in February 2006 for planned conversion to integrated tug-barge.

RIDGETOWN
- Last sailed for Upper Lakes Shipping, Toronto, Ontario
- Lake bulk freighter

Built: Chicago Shipbuilding Co., Chicago, Illinois, 1905
Length: 569'
Beam: 31'
Depth: 00'
Capacity at mid-summer draft: 000 tons
Propulsion: steam
Engine/Horsepower: 1800-i.h.p. triple expansion steam engine built by American Ship Building Co., Cleveland, Ohio
Lineage:
- 1905–1963: *William E. Cory*, Pittsburgh Steamship Co., Cleveland, Ohio
- 1963–1970: *Ridgetown*, Upper Lakes Shipping Co., Toronto, Ontario
- 1970–1974: *Ridgetown*, Canadian Dredge & Dry Dock Co., Toronto, Ontario (not active)

Notes: Built by Chicago Shipbuilding Co., Chicago, Illinois, in 1905 as Pittsburgh Steamship Co., *William E. Corey*. Laid-up at Duluth in 1960, sold in 1963 to Upper Lakes Shipping and named *Ridgetown*. Laid-up in Toronto November 17, 1969; sold May 1970 to Canadian Dredge & Dry Dock Co., Toronto, Ontario, and used as temporary break wall during construction of Ontario Hydro power plant at Nanticoke, Ontario. Returned to Toronto September 1973. Relocated to Port Credit, Ontario, loaded with stone and sunk as permanent break wall June 21, 1974.

EDWARD L. RYERSON
- Indiana Harbor Steamship Co., managed by Central Marine Logistics, Highland, Indiana
- Straight-deck bulk carrier

Built: Manitowoc Shipbuilding Co., Manitowoc, Wisconsin, 1960
Length: 730'

Beam: 75'
Depth: 39'
Capacity at mid-summer draft: 27,500 tons
Propulsion: steam turbine
Engine/Horsepower: 9900 s.h.p., cross-compound steam turbine built by General Electric Co., Schenectady, New York.
Lineage:

- 1960–1998: *Edward L. Ryerson*, Inland Steel Co., Chicago, Illinois
- 1998–present: *Edward L. Ryerson*, Indiana Harbor Steamship Co., managed by Central Marine Logistics, Highland, Indiana

Notes: *Edward L. Ryerson* constructed for Inland Steel by Manitowoc Shipbuilding Co., Manitowoc, Wisconsin, and launched January 21, 1960. Last steam-powered U.S.-flagged laker built; last U.S.-flagged straight-decker built; last laker built by Manitowoc Shipbuilding. Laid-up frequently for entire seasons during late 1980s and 1990s; did not sail during 1986 and 1987 seasons, nor during 1994–1996 seasons. Reactivated April 5, 1997, but returned to long-term lay-up at Bay Shipbuilding, Sturgeon bay, Wisconsin, December 12, 1998. Sale of Inland Steel to Ispat International of the Netherlands in 1998 resulted in transfer of vessel to Indiana Harbor Steamship Co., under management Central Marine Logistics, Highland, Indiana. Returned to duty June 3, 2006, only U.S.-flagged straight-decker in active service. Laid up at Superior, Wisc., May 18, 2009.

ST. MARYS CHALLENGER

- St. Marys Cement (Port City Marine Services, Muskegon, Mich.)
- Cement carrier

Built: Great Lakes Engineering Works, Ecorse, Michigan, 1906
Length: 551' 1"
Beam: 56'
Depth: 31'
Capacity at mid-summer draft: 10,250 tons
Propulsion: steam
Engine/horsepower (1906–1950): 1665 i.h.p., triple-expansion, Great Lakes Engineering Works, Ecorse, Michigan
Engine/horsepower (1950–2013): 3500 i.h.p., 4-cylinder Skinner Marine Unaflow, Skinner Engine Co., Erie, Pennsylvania
Lineage:

- 1906–1926: *William P. Snyder*, Shenango Furnace Co., Cleveland, Ohio
- 1926–1929: *Elton Hoyt II*, Stewart Furnace Co., Cleveland, Ohio
- 1929–1930: *Elton Hoyt II*, Youngstown Steamship Co., Cleveland, Ohio
- 1930–1952: *Elton Hoyt II* (1st), Interlake Steamship Co., Cleveland, Ohio
- 1952–1966: *Alex D. Chisholm*, Interlake Steamship Co., Cleveland, Ohio

- 1966–1999: *Medusa Challenger*, Cement Transit Co., (division of Medusa Portland Cement), Detroit, Michigan
- 1999–2005: *Southdown Challenger*, Southdown Inc., then Wilmington Trust, Wilmington, Delaware; operated by HMC Ship Management Ltd., Lemont, Illinois
- 2005–2013: *St. Marys Challenger,* St. Marys Cement Inc., Detroit, Michigan, operated by HMC Ship Management Ltd., Lemont, Illinois until [date]. Operated by Port City Steamship Services, Muskegon, Mich., until retirement in November 2013.

Notes: *William P. Snyder* launched by Great Lakes Engineering Works, Ecorse, Michigan, on February 7, 1906. Sold to Stewart Furnace Co., June 26, 1926 and renamed *Elton Hoyt II*. Owned briefly by Youngstown Steamship, 1929–30, then sold to Interlake Steamship Co. Re-powered with 3500-i.h.p., 4-cylinder Skinner Marine Unaflow reciprocating steam engine and outfitted with new boilers in 1950. Renamed *Alex D, Chisholm* in 1952. Purchased by Medusa Portland Cement Co., in 1966; converted to cement carrier by Manitowoc Shipbuilding Co., Manitowoc, Wisconsin and christened *Medusa Challenger*. Southdown Inc., acquired Medusa Cement in 1998; vessel renamed *Southdown Challenger* at Milwaukee, Wisconsin, in April 1999. Title transferred to Wilmington Trust, Wilmington, Delaware, with Southdown acquisition by Cemex in 2000; vessel operated by HMC Ship Management Ltd., Lemont, Illinois. Cemex acquired by Votorantim Cimentos of Brazil in 2005; vessel transferred to subsidiary St. Marys Cement Inc., and renamed *St. Marys Challenger* in April 2005. Celebrated 100th year in Great Lakes service in 2006. Retired after arrival at Bay Shipbuilding Co., Sturgeon Bay, Wisc., under her own power on November 11, 2013. Converted to barge in 2014.

SAGINAW

- Lower Lakes Towing Co., Port Dover, Ontario
- Self-unloader

Built: Manitowoc Shipbuilding Co., Manitowoc, Wisconsin, 1953
Length: 639' 3"
Beam: 72'
Depth: 36'
Capacity at mid-summer draft: 20,200 tons
Propulsion: diesel
Engine/horsepower — original: 7700 s.h.p. steam turbine; DeLaval Steam Turbine Co., Trenton, New Jersey
Engine/horsepower — current: 8160 b.h.p., 6-cylinder MaK 6M43C diesel
Lineage:

- 1953–1999: *John J. Boland*, American Steamship Co., Buffalo, New York
- 1999–present: *Saginaw*, Lower Lakes Towing Co., Port Dover, Ontario

Notes: Built as *John J. Boland* for American Steamship Co., Buffalo, N.Y. Launched at Manitowoc Shipbuilding on May 3, 1953. Laid-up at Superior, Wisconsin, December 27, 1998 and did not sail during 1999 season. Sold to Lower Lakes Towing Co., Port Dover, Ontario, October 22, 1999. Christened *Saginaw* at Sarnia, Ontario, November 20, 1999. Converted to diesel during winter lay up at Sarnia, Ontario, in early 2008. Returned to service in June 2008, powered by 8160- b.h.p, 6-cylinder, MaK 6M43C diesel engine.

SEAWAY QUEEN

- Upper Lakes Shipping, Toronto, Ontario
- Straight-deck bulk carrier

Built: Port Weller Dry Docks Ltd., St. Catharines, Ontario, 1959
Length: 713' 3"
Beam: 72'
Depth: 37'
Capacity at mid-summer draft: 24,300 tons
Propulsion: steam turbine
Engine/Horsepower: 8250-s.h.p. steam turbine built by John Inglis Co., Toronto, Ontario
Lineage:

- 1959–2004: *Seaway Queen*, Upper Lakes Shipping, Toronto, Ontario

Notes: Built by Port Weller Dry Docks Ltd., St. Catharines, Ontario, and christened Upper Lakes Shipping *Seaway Queen*, May 30, 1959. Spent entire career operating under Upper Lakes flag. Laid-up at Toronto, Ontario, in 1999. Sold for scrap and towed to Alang, India, October 2003.

J.W. SHELLEY

- Vanguard Shipping Ltd., Ingleside, Ontario
- Straight-deck bulk carrier

Built: Collingwood Shipyards, Collingwood, Ontario, 1968
Length: 730'
Beam: 75'
Depth: 39' 8"
Capacity at mid-summer draft: 26,666 tons
Propulsion: diesel
Engine/Horsepower: 8,000 b.h.p., from four 12-cylinder, 2000 b.h.p. Fairbanks-Morse 38D 8 1/8 opposed-piston engines
Lineage:

- 1968–2005: *Algocen*, Algoma Central Corporation, Sault Ste. Marie, Ontario.
- 2005–2008: *Valgocen*, Recyling Technologies, New Jersey (for storage hull)
- 2008–2012: *J.W. Shelley*, Vanguard Shipping Ltd., Ingleside, Ontario
- 2012–2013: *Phoenix Star,* T.F. Warren Group, Brantford, Ontario

Notes: Built by Collingwood Shipyards, Collingwood, Ontario, September 20, 1968. Last traditional straight-deck bulk carrier built at Collingwood. Laid up at Montreal, Quebec, January 4, 2005; sold to Recycling Technologies and towed to Keasbey, New Jersey ,for use as a storage hull. Sold to Vanguard Shipping Ltd., of Ingleside, Ontario, May 2008 and re-registered as *J.W. Shelley*. Moved to Brooklyn, New York for repairs and sailed under her own power to Montreal, Quebec, arriving September 5, 2008, for customs clearance and Seaway inspection. Departed Montreal September 6, 2008 to load grain at Superior, Wisconsin. Sold to T.F. Warren Group, Brantford, Ontario, in July 2012 and christened *Phoenix Star*. Laid up for repairs and five-year survey at Ironhead Shipyard, December 19, 2012. Sold in bankruptcy to Ironhead after repairs to damage suffered in earlier grounding proved to be greater than anticipated. Scrapped by Ironhead in June 2013.

JOHN SHERWIN
- Lakes Shipping Co., division of Interlake Steamship Co., Richfield, Ohio
- Self-unloader

Built: American Ship Building, Toledo, Ohio, 1958
Length: 806' (lengthened from 710')
Beam: 75'
Depth: 37' 6"
Capacity at mid-summer draft: 31,500 tons
Propulsion: steam turbine
Engine/Horsepower: 9350 s.h.p., cross-compound steam turbine built by DeLaval Steam Turbine Co., Trenton, New Jersey.
Lineage:
- 1958–2006: *John Sherwin*, Lakes Shipping Co., division of Interlake Steamship Co., Richfield, Ohio

Notes: Built by American Ship Building, Toledo, Ohio, for Interlake Steamship Co., in 1957–58 and christened *John Sherwin* at Cleveland, Ohio, May 1, 1958. Modifications performed during winter 1972–73 at Fraser Shipyards, Superior, Wisconsin, included lengthening of hull from 710 to 806 feet and conversion of boilers from coal-burning to oil-fired operation. Laid-up at Superior, Wisconsin, November 16, 1981. Moved in September 2006, after 25 years in lay-up at Superior, to South Chicago, Illinois, for use as storage hull. Moved to Bay Shipbuilding, Sturgeon Bay, Wisc., in 2008 for planned conversion to diesel and re-activation. Work cancelled and vessel moved to long term lay-up at De Tour, Mich.

SOUTHDOWN CHALLENGER
— see St. Marys Challenger

S.S. SPARTAN
- Lake Michigan Carferry Service Inc., Ludington, Michigan
- Car ferry

Built: Christy Corporation, Sturgeon Bay, Wisconsin, 1952
Length: 410' 6"
Beam: 59' 6"
Depth: 24'
Capacity: 520 passengers, 180 automobiles
Propulsion: steam
Engine/Horsepower: 7000 b.h.p. from two 3500-i.h.p., steeple-compound, 4-cylinder Skinner Marine Unaflow engines built by Skinner Engine Co., Erie, Pennsylvania
Lineage:
- 1952–1983: S.S. *Spartan*, Chesapeake & Ohio Railway
- 1983–1991: S.S. *Spartan*, Wisconsin-Michigan Transportation Co. Out of service.
- 1991–present: S.S. *Badger*, Lake Michigan Carferry Service Inc., Ludington, Michigan. Not in service.

Notes: S.S. *Spartan* built for Chesapeake & Ohio Railway Lake Michigan car ferry service by Christy Corporation, Sturgeon Bay, Wisconsin. Launched in January 1952 and operated in car ferry service transporting rail cars, motor vehicles and passengers between Ludington Michigan, and Milwaukee, Manitowoc and Kewaunee, Wisconsin. Laid-up at Ludington, Michigan, January 20, 1979. Included in transactions with sale of *Badger* to Wisconsin-Michigan Transportation Co., in 1983 and Lake Michigan Carferry Service in 1991, but has remained out of service since 1979.

MYRON C. TAYLOR — see Calumet

CSL TADOUSSAC
- Canada Steamship Lines, Montreal, Quebec
- Self-unloader

Built: Collingwood Shipyards, Collingwood, Onatrio, 1969
Length: 730'
Beam: 77', 11"
Depth: 42'
Capacity at mid-summer draft: 30, 051 tons
Propulsion: diesel
Engine/horsepower: 9600 b.h.p., 6-cylinder Sulzer 6RND76 supplied by Sulzer Bros., Ltd., Winterhur, Switzerland
Lineage:
- 1969–2001: *Tadoussac*, Canada Steamship Lines, Montreal, Quebec
- 2001–present: *CSL Tadoussac*, Canada Steamship Lines, Montreal, Quebec

Notes:
Built at Collingwood Shipyards as Canada Steamship Lines *Tadoussac*, the last CSL vessel constructed with traditional forward pilothouse. Rebuilt with in winter 2001 with new, wider mid-section at Port Weller Dry Docks, St. Catharines, Ontario. Rechristened *CSL Tadoussac* in ceremony at Port Weller March 3, 2001.

Stack detail, *Saginaw*, September 2005.

VOYAGEUR INDEPENDENT — see Ojibway

Reference sources: This data is compiled with information provided by shipping companies, as well as from a number of indispensable reference sources: *Moran's Shoreside Companion for Great Lakes Ships*, William P. Moran; *Know Your Ships*, Roger LeLievre; *The Marine Historical Society of Detroit's Ahoy and Farewell* series of books, and from George Wharton's vessel histories included on the invaluable Great Lakes and Seaway Shipping site at www.boatnerd.com.

INDEX